TEST SUCCESS

Test-Taking and Study Strategies for All Students, Including Those with ADD and LD

By Blythe Grossberg, Psy.D.

Illustrated by Peter Welleman

For Middle School, High School and First-Year College Students

For more information please contact the publisher.

Specialty Press. Inc.
300 N.W. 70th Avenue, Suite 102
Plantation, Florida 33317
(954) 792-8100 • (800) 233-9273
www.addwarehouse.com

Library of Congress Cataloging-in-Publication Data.

Grossberg, Blythe N.

Test Success: Test-Taking and Study Strategies for All Students,

Including Those with ADD and LD / Blythe Grossberg.

        p. cm.

ISBN 978-1-886941-72-4 (alk. paper)

1. Test-taking skills—Juvenile literature. 2. Examinations—Study guides—Juvenile literature. I. Title.

LB3060.57.G76 2009

371.26–dc22

                    2008034179

About the Author

Blythe Grossberg, Psy.D., is the Upper School learning specialist at the Collegiate School in New York City. She has worked with students in grades 5-12 to help them be more effective at school. Her previous book is "Making ADD Work: On-the-Job Strategies for Coping with Attention Deficit Disorder" (Perigee, 2005).

Table of Contents

1 Shopping for a Learning Style

Discover Your Learning Style

    Shop for Your Style: Are You an Auditory, Visual, or Kinesthetic Learner?

Customize Your Study Techniques

Special Study Strategies for Athletes, Artists, Musicians, and Actors

Real-life Strategies

9 Beating the Clock: Time-Management Strategies

Developing a Study Schedule

The Top Ten Obstacles to Studying and How to Defeat Them

Real-life Strategies

19 Playing and Winning the Testing "Game"

"Psyching Out" the Test—and Your Teacher

Maintaining Focus and Concentration While Studying

    A Note on Medication

How to Calm Down and Not Rush

    A Note on Bubbling in Answers

Is There Any Way to Enjoy Studying?

Real-life Strategies

33 Becoming Jane Austen: Acing Essay Tests

Preparing for Essay Tests

Sample Essay

After Writing: Attending to Grammar, Handwriting, and Organization

Essay Writing Checklist

Improving Your Vocabulary

Pacing

Real-life Strategies

41 Einstein Made Easy: Outwitting Math Tests

Studying for Math Tests

Avoiding Careless Mistakes

Dealing with "Math Anxiety" and Avoiding Rushing

Real-life Strategies

47 Useful for *Jeopardy*: Mastering Tests that Require Memorization

Preparing for History Tests

    Sample History Study Guide

    Sample History Notes

How to Study for Science Tests

Studying for Foreign Language Tests: Vocabulary, Grammar, and Reading
Real-life Strategies

57 Taking the Sting out of Pop Quizzes
How to Be Prepared
Maintaining Your Cool
Improving Your Results on Pop Quizzes
Real-life Strategies

59 Winning the Guessing Game: How to Take Multiple-Choice Tests
Eliminate the Negative
Reading Between the Lines
Real-life Strategies

63 Standardized Tests: State-Mandated Tests and College-Entrance Tests
Establishing a Study Schedule
Pacing on the Test
How to Calm Down and Not Rush
   A Note on Bubbling in Answers
   A Note on Medication
Gaining Confidence and Overcoming Procrastination
Real-life Strategies

67 Getting and Using Accommodations in School
Which Accommodations are Right for You?
Using Your Accommodations Wisely
Applying for Accommodations on College-Entrance Exams: the SAT and ACT
Real-life Strategies

73 Using Your Results to Improve
How to Use Your Results to Get Better
Analysis of Mistakes and Strategies to Correct Them
Getting Your Parents off Your Back
How to Work with Teachers and Tutors
Real-life Strategies

77 Helpful Books and Websites

79 Summary of What I Learned from this Book

81 Teacher Worksheets and Classroom Exercises

Chapter One:
Shopping for a Learning Style

Discover Your Learning Style: Finding the Perfect Fit

This book starts with a shopping expedition. You'll get to try on different learning styles and decide which one suits you best. Instead of finding the best fit for a new pair of sneakers, you'll be looking for the way of studying that's the most natural to you. Just as you feel most comfortable in the pair of shoes that conforms best to your foot, you'll feel the most comfortable studying for tests if you find the way of learning that conforms to the way your mind works. The idea behind shopping for a learning style is that you can bring a lot of yourself to the process of studying for and taking tests. Throughout this book, you will find strategies that work for you. You can pick and choose the tips that you think will work, and you don't have to try those you think aren't right for you.

Make sense of your senses:
Understanding how you primarily take in information.

The first step in customizing the way you learn is to understand how you take in information. People vary in which sense they prioritize when absorbing new material. Some people remember information best when they see it. These types of learners are **visual** in nature. Other people are **auditory** learners who tend to recall information that they hear—these are the types of students who often compose songs to study for tests. Finally, there are students who are **kinesthetic** and have to use their bodies to act out information. They remember best what they do—not what they see or hear.

We of course use all our senses all the time, but we may favor one over the other. To understand which type of learner you are, start by taking this short test. Don't worry—this is the fun sort of test that tells you more about yourself (and what could be more interesting?). After the test, you'll learn how to use your primary sense to make studying more interesting and to recall the information with greater ease.

SHOP FOR YOUR STYLE:
Are you an auditory, visual, or kinesthetic learner?
Place a check mark next to the statements that describe you.

Auditory learners:

_____ I remember words when they are put to a beat or to music.

_____ I remember material that I hear presented aloud without taking any notes.

_____ I prefer spoken directions over written directions.

_____ I don't often understand diagrams or graphs without an explanation.

_____ I like to talk through problems.

Visual Learners:

_____ I prefer written directions rather than oral directions.

_____ I like to take notes to understand material.

_____ I understand graphs and charts.

_____ I remember what I read.

_____ I like to use color to remember material.

Kinesthetic Learners:

_____ I'm good at building objects.

_____ I can put together puzzles easily.

_____ I'm constantly gesturing with my hands.

____ **Once I do an activity, I remember how to do it.**

____ **I don't often remember what was said or seen.**

Count up the number of check marks.

Auditory: ____

Visual: ____

Kinesthetic: ____

Which type of learner are you? _____

Does this news surprise you? _____

Read below to find out more about your learning style and how to use your style to make studying easier and more enjoyable. If you have two primary learning styles or one primary learning style with a close second, read the potential strategies for both styles.

CUSTOMIZE YOUR STUDY TECHNIQUES

Auditory Learners

If you are primarily an auditory learner, you need to hear material to remember it. You may enjoy music, and putting information into the form of a song may help you recall it. In school, you may be the kind of student who has to hear the information presented aloud in class to have it stick in your mind. Discussion-oriented classes may help you retain the material, and you may find yourself playing through what was said in class as if it were a soundtrack.

Here are some techniques that can help you learn in the classroom and study at home. Place check marks next to those you think will help you:

____ Make up songs to remember material, such as historical dates or vocabulary words.

____ Talk through information, or engage in a discussion about the material.

____ Listen to books on tape, which are available at stores or through Recordings for the Blind and Dyslexic (see "Helpful Books and Websites" at the end of the book).

____ Repeat information aloud for as many times as it takes you to remember it.

____ Use language to explain complicated graphs or diagrams.

____ Record classes (if acceptable to your teacher) and play them back while studying.

____ Use your iPod or MP3 Player to record material and listen to it repeatedly.

Visual Learners:

If you are a visual learner, you recall what you see. You most likely learn well when teachers write information on the board, and when you take notes. You need to make study guides that involve writing out the material. In addition, you can use tools such as ***semantic maps*** that make visual connections between different parts of the material. Here is a simple kind of semantic map of the U.S. federal court system:

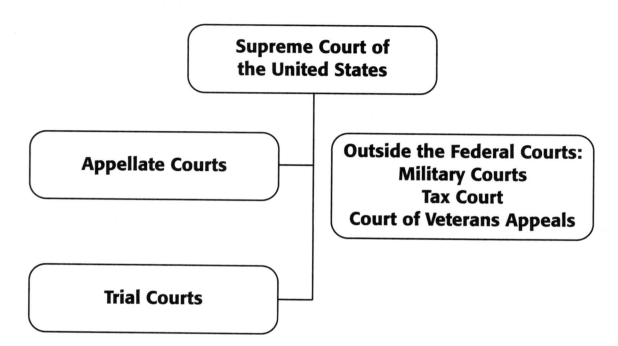

This so-called semantic map shows the connections between different concepts—in this case, the organization of different courts. The diagram helps you make visual connections that reinforce what you know. You can draw these types of charts yourself while studying, or you can use a software program such as Inspiration (available online at inspiration.com) to help you.

Color may also help you remember information. For example, you can use different-colored flash cards to recall information. If you are trying to remember vocabulary words, you can make all nouns red, all verbs blue, and all adjectives yellow.

Here is a list of some techniques that build on a visual learning style:

_____ Use a program such as Inspiration (available online at inspiration.com) to map out material.

_____ Make your own semantic map (see the example above) to draw relationships between parts of the material you need to know.

_____ Integrate color into your studying: for example, use different colors for words of different parts of speech.

_____ Use different colored highlighter pens when you are annotating, or taking notes on your reading.

_____ Use charts and flash cards.

_____ Be sure to take notes during class, and use them to study.

3" x 5" Index Card

(WORD)

mottled

FRONT

(PART OF SPEECH) adj.

(DEFINITION) spotted or
              blotched in color

(SENTENCE)   The owl had
<u>mottled</u> coloring that allowed it to
blend in with the tree.

BACK

Kinesthetic Learners

If you are a kinesthetic learner, you learn by doing. You need to use your hands or your body to act out information or to put things together. You may enjoy building things and doing sports. In the earlier grades, it's easier to use your kinesthetic sense. You can work on arts and crafts and drama projects such as posters, performances, and dioramas. You are most likely the star of plays, science fairs, art classes, and the sports field.

However, as you get into middle and high school, you may find it more difficult to use your kinesthetic sense. You may find it difficult even to sit still in the classroom, as you tend to learn by walking around. Unlike in the classroom, however, you can use different study techniques at home that build on your kinesthetic style. Here are some potential study strategies:

_____ Act out the information. Pretend, for example, that you are a figure in history or a famous scientist you are studying.

_____ Make art work or a physical object related to the material you are studying, such as a model of a volcano or the solar system.

_____ Walk around while studying. You can even study different subjects in different rooms of your school or house so you recall the information when you're in that room. Try studying in the classroom where you will take a test.

_____ Post information on your walls and shoot a soft ball at it while reciting it aloud.

_____ Use flash cards that you build with, shuffle, and arrange on your desk or floor.

Special Study Strategies for Athletes, Artists, Musicians, and Actors

If you are an athlete, artist, musician, or actor, you have special talents that you are accustomed to using outside the classroom. What you may not know is that you can use your talents to study for tests to make your preparation more effective and fun.

Music to your ears.

If you are a musician, your ears can help you not only in music class but in all your work. Your teacher may not be musical, but you can rearrange the material you are studying to make it more musical in nature. You are most likely an auditory learner (see the section above), and you learn best by putting material to music. Have you ever written a song about the material you are studying? You might try this technique and the others that follow to help you make your studying more enjoyable and productive.

> _____ Listen to familiar music as you study. Think of this music when you are taking a test to make the material come back to you.

> _____ Rearrange material so that you can make rhymes or jingles out of it. Then sing it to yourself or put it to music.

> _____ Record classroom discussions (if acceptable to your teacher) and play them back while listening to soft music in the background.

Real-life strategy: Jake, a guitar player, had a hard time memorizing vocabulary terms in biology until he recorded them and put them onto his iPod. He listened to them many times on the way to and from school until he had them firmly in his head. In addition, his teacher realized that Jake would understand the biology multiple-choice test questions better if she read them aloud to Jake. Once Jake heard the questions aloud, he was able to answer them more correctly and recall what he knew. These strategies boosted his grade in biology and gave Jake more confidence and a greater willingness to use this technique to study French vocabulary words using his iPod as well.

Acting out.

"All the world's a stage," wrote Shakespeare. If you enjoy acting, you can use your craft while studying. Acting is a complete sensory experience in which you use your body, voice, and emotions before the audience. You can use these same senses to encode, or store, information for school. Actors also tend to be good at remembering their lines, and their minds have been honed to recall a lot of verbal information. You can use this gift while studying. Some of the actors I've met have been able to recite long strings of information backward and forward because they've developed techniques for memorizing lines. For example, some actors imagine words or scenes in their heads, while others need to recite their lines out loud before a mirror to remember them. The following are some strategies adapted from the stage that you can also use at your desk:

_____ Read the information from your textbook or notes out loud in a dramatic voice before the mirror. Use the appropriate physical expressions and facial gestures. For example, if you are studying information about how the Soviets were angry at Americans for possessing the atomic bomb during the Cold War, adopt a menacing tone and a threatening grimace.

_____ Read the information from your textbook or class notes back and forth with a friend. You are used to memorizing dialogue, and reading the information with a partner will allow you to use your ability to recall other people's lines, as well as your own, from hearing them spoken aloud.

_____ Build on the same technique you use to memorize your lines to memorize information for school. If you tend to picture your lines in your head, for example, use the same technique to memorize material for tests.

_____ Without going overboard and becoming a total ham, you can be a bit dramatic in class. While listening in class, use your actors' techniques to respond to the teachers' comments with physical gestures.

Scoring points on and off the field.

Athletes can use the determination and drive they have on the field in the classroom. If you are an athlete, you understand the value of the drill—of repeating the same skill again and again until you get it right. You can use your willingness to practice, your ability to concentrate, and your love of the game to do well in school. You are also most likely able to come up with a play—whether it's a soccer goal or a basket or an ace—in a clutch moment. Your ability to stay focused when the game is on the line can help you on test day as well as on game day. These strategies build on the athlete's temperament and willingness to work hard:

_____ Use your patience to practice drills on and off the field. Just as you would practice a foul shot again and again, you can use the same types of drills to remember information. Quiz yourself repeatedly about information by shuffling through flash cards. For each card you miss, make yourself practice it again and again until you get it right.

_____ Put your whole self into studying, and use your game to study. For example, place vocabulary words or flash cards with the information you need to know (historical names and dates, math formulas, etc.) on the back of a basketball hoop and shoot baskets at it until you remember it. You can also kick a soccer ball against an outside wall with the information on it.

_____ Use the same techniques you've perfected to stay calm during a key moment in a game—whether it's shooting a foul shot, kicking a penalty shot, or batting when you have two strikes—to stay clear and focused during a test.

_____ Plan your studying time so that you are not too tired; after a difficult game, you may be too worn out to pay attention to studying. Instead, before studying, you may want to do some light exercise—such as a short run or twenty minutes outside kicking a soccer ball—to help keep you relaxed and alert.

Make an art out of studying.

If you are an artist, you can put your artistic skills to work making the information you need to know for school more beautiful and easier to understand. When you are studying, take out your colored pencils and markers and use color and illustrations to accompany written words. Artists tend to think in creative, non-linear ways (meaning that they don't always go directly from point A to B but enjoy diversions along the way), and the strategies below may help rearrange material creatively to make it more enjoyable and comprehensible:

_____ Use color for flash cards or for any material that has different parts—such as different parts of speech, masculine and feminine words in foreign languages, different operations in math, different parts of the body in biology, etc.

_____ Draw material, when possible, instead of reading it. For example, you can draw a chart of the respiratory system instead of reading about it in a textbook.

_____ Use semantic maps (see the example above) to make connections between material. For example, if you are studying the organization of the U.S. court system, draw each type of court in a bubble and connect them in terms of their hierarchy or importance using arrows.

_____ Illustrate scenes in books that you are reading. Drawing a detailed scene will help you remember the characters' personality, mood, setting, and plot.

Check-in:

My primary learning style is _____: (kinesthetic, visual, or auditory)

If I have a close second, it is:_____

Write down the top five study techniques from this chapter that you think will help you.

_____

_____

_____

_____

Chapter 2:
<u>Beating the Clock: Time-Management Strategies</u>

Developing a Study Schedule

If Procrastination were a class, most students would receive an A+. They have mastered the art of IMing, surfing the Web, going on to Facebook, talking on the phone, playing World of Warcraft, and just staring into space instead of studying. After a day of classes, after-school activities, sports, and work, very few students have the mental fire-power left to burn the midnight oil preparing for tests. That's why it's critical to break up your studying over time and use the moments you have to the fullest. You want to make sure to capitalize on the times you feel energized to fit in a few minutes of high-quality work. If you study when you are alert, you will find that you are more productive, saving you precious moments to devote to watching your favorite shows and IMing your friends.

Here's the main rule about studying:

Tip#1: Break down your studying into small, manageable bits.

While you may want to procrastinate as much as possible, you will actually feel less pain if you divide the bitter pill of studying into smaller units of time. If you study when you are better rested, you will also make better use of each minute, allowing yourself to have free time to devote to worthier pursuits, such as video games and Facebook.

Studies have shown that cramming the night before an exam is not effective for the vast majority of students. Your mind needs time to process new information, and while some lucky students are fortunate enough to be able to cram and do well, most are not able to study all the material the night before a big test. Some tests—such as those in history and science—require such a great deal of memorization that students need to work on familiarizing themselves with the material over several nights. The night before the test should be reserved for mastering last-minute details, integrating or putting together the material, and getting a good night's sleep to be fresh on the test day.

Tip #2: Use a planner to break down your studying time.

It is important to have a weekly time during which you sit down and enter all your assignments into an organizing device—whether it's a weekly planner or an electronic device such as a Treo or BlackBerry. Once you enter your assignments into your planner, you can start backdating—or breaking down your work day by day to make sure you are prepared well in advance of the test day.

When you plan your studying for a test, consider all the smaller tasks involved in preparing thoroughly for the test. Take this example of how a student could prepare for a science test on volcanoes:

a. Review chapters 2-3 (pages 90-105) in the textbook; take notes.

b. Answer the review questions at the end of each chapter.

c. Review class notes from November 2, 3, 5, 6, and 9th. Underline key terms.

d. Review notes from class movie on volcanoes.

e. Get missing class notes from November 10, when I was absent.

f. Read over Ms. Smith's review sheet and make sure I know the material.

WEEKLY SCHEDULE SHEET   WEEK OF 3/2

TIME	MONDAY	TUESDAY	WEDNESDAY	THURSDAY	FRIDAY	SATURDAY	SUNDAY
4:00 - 5:00 or earlier	volleyball practice	club meeting	volleyball practice	dentist	bring home math sheets for review	volleyball game	
5:00 - 5:30	review Spanish verbs for quiz						read English p.110-120
5:30 - 6:00	↑ dinner	↓	↓	email team about Sat.		↓	and annotate
6:00 - 6:30	↓	dinner	dinner	dinner			Spanish cable show on
6:30 - 7:00	math:p.121 #3-11	math:p.123 #4-23	review science notes				
7:00 - 7:30	read history (150-175)+	read science notes	make science study guide	review history notes from week			review math study guide
7:30 - 8:00	take notes	read science handout - test Thursday	break	review Spanish verbs			
8:00 - 8:30	break	relax	read English p.95-110	prepare for math review class	movies		organize next week's work
8:30 - 9:00	call Sam to get notes		+ annotate	tomorrow ↓			
9:00 - 9:30	TV, relax		bed				
9:30 - 10:00	↓	↓				↓	
10:00 - 10:30 or after							
AVAILABLE TIME / TIME USED FOR STUDY	3 hrs.	1.5 hrs.	2 hrs.	2 hrs.			3 hrs.

See how this student used her planner to break down studying for the test:
- Monday: Call Julia to get missing class notes; read over pp. 90-100 (30 minutes)
- Tuesday: Read pp. 100-105, read and highlight notes from Nov. 2, 3, 5 (45 minutes)
- Wednesday: Read and highlight notes from Nov. 6, 9, 10; review movie notes (45 minutes). Prepare list of questions to ask Ms. Smith during review period tomorrow.
- Thursday: Read over review sheet and review earlier notes. (30 minutes): watch favorite television show and go to bed early
- Friday: Test.

Be sure to notice that this student makes a plan to study during the entire week to prepare for her test on Friday. Planning ahead allows her to collect missing materials (such as class notes from a friend to make up for a day on which she was absent) and to prepare questions to ask during a class review session. In addition, she plans to study for two-and-a-half hours over several nights rather than studying for several hours on one night. This schedule allows her to watch her favorite television show on Thursday night and to go to bed early and be well-rested on the day of the test.

CHECK-IN: Do you have a planner or an organizational tool that helps you plan your work?

_____

_____

_____

_____

Tip #3: Be flexible about scheduling your time using a nightly to-do list.

Some students attempt to make a study schedule but feel defeated when they can't follow it to the letter. They then give up trying to schedule their time at all and resign themselves to procrastination and last-minute cramming. If you have been guilty of such practices, don't despair. You may be helped by allowing yourself a more flexible schedule that is firm but allows for the inevitable slip-ups and disruptions. The idea is to schedule more time than you need at first so that if something happens to prevent you from living up to it, the whole structure doesn't fall apart.

Say, for example, that you have a math test on Thursday. It's Sunday night, and you are planning out your week. If you think you will require two solid sessions of one hour each to prepare for the test, schedule time for Monday, Tuesday, and Wednesday nights. That way, even if you have more homework than you expected on Tuesday and can't get to studying, you will still have time on Wednesday. Don't fall victim to "magical thinking"—the idea that you will always do exactly what your schedule says. Allow for some wiggle room and some human error. That way, you will still be able to keep on track.

You can make copies of the blank to-do list included in the back of this book. Each night, use the to-do list to list each task you have to complete. Then, number the list in order of the way you will complete the tasks. Put a rough estimate of how much time each task will take. Then, check the tasks off once you complete them. Tasks you haven't yet completed can be transferred to the next night's list.

Real-life strategy: Daniel, a 7th grader who has ADD and struggles to plan his study time, disagreed with his parents and teachers about the need to set up a structured study schedule. His teachers helped him set up schedules to prepare for upcoming tests, but he found he could never stick to them. As a result, he would get frustrated and decide to throw away the study schedule entirely. Only when he realized that he could approach the schedule with some flexibility did he start to understand that a structured study schedule would help him. He now makes a plan for each of several days before a test and tries to finish what he can. If he doesn't finish everything, he pushes his unfinished work to the next day. He also builds in extra time, such as an extra study session, to make sure that in case he doesn't get to everything he needs to on one day, he has the next day to make up the work he didn't get to.

GET IT DONE TODAY

Date __3/2__

Priority	Assignment	Date Due	Completed
5	Review French vocabulary (10 cards)	3/4	☐
1	Read pp. 120-135 in science book	3/3	☑
2	Answer questions #1-5 in science	3/3	☑
7	Call Madeline for classnotes: 2/28	3/5	☐
3	Pack gym bag for tomorrow	3/3	☐
4	print out missing history questions	3/3	☐
6	review grammar for quiz on Friday	3/6	☐
			☐
			☐
			☐
			☐
			☐
			☐

Tip #4: Get energized to study.

Adults—namely parents and teachers--are often guilty of forgetting how exhausting it is to be a kid. Not only do you have to go to school for seven or so hours a day, you also have to participate in sports, gym, after-school activities; deal with your friends; do your chores; and then come home to a night of homework. An adult might feel inclined to quit a job that required so much work! Nonetheless, you have no choice but to take it on—even though you may also be growing and feeling tired every minute of the day. Never mind that childhood is supposed to be the time for fun and relaxation!

Students often make the mistake of forgetting how tired they are. They think they can realistically go home after a soccer game and study for a difficult biology test, and they forget that the brain requires rest, relaxation, and energy to work well—just like muscles. Your body needs a day after a hard game to return to itself, and you need time for your mind to recover after school in order to take on your work and serious studying. Don't get me wrong—you don't have an excuse to kick back and do nothing and waste hours playing video games or chatting with your friends when you have a ton of homework to do. However, you may want to get your brain refreshed and awakened for conscientious studying by doing the following:

- take a jog of 20-30 minutes
- listen to relaxing music for a few minutes
- take a short nap of about 20 minutes—longer naps will most likely make you feel even groggier and more exhausted, but a short nap will refresh you

BRAINSTORM: What are your ways to wake up and refresh yourself before studying?

_____

_____

_____

Medication

If you take medication for ADD, you may want to work with your doctor to be sure that you are feeling awake during your studying and homework time. Many students find that even longer-acting ADD medication wears off by the afternoon—just at the time they sit down to study. You should consult your doctor to be sure that your medication is covering not only the school day, but also the time you need to concentrate while studying. Be sure to tell your doctor about any other symptoms you have related to ADD medication that affect your ability to get your studying done and to feel alert while doing so.

Real-Life Strategy: When William started taking medication to treat his ADD in the 6th grade, it helped him concentrate in school. He felt more alert in class, and his grades improved. He didn't have more than a hour of homework each night, so he found that he could do his work at home without taking additional medication. However, when he entered the 7th grade, he found that his homework became more demanding and time-consuming. While he once had only an hour of work at night, he now easily had two, and his medication usually had worn off by the time he sat down to do his homework. He and his parents consulted his family physician, who had prescribed the medication, and they worked out a smaller dose that he could take at 4 to help him with his work. William continued to consult his physician during his 7th grade year to make sure that his dose was accurate and safe, and he found that his homework went more smoothly and he was more efficient.

Tip #5: Reward yourself.

Rewards are a crucial part of studying. Building small rewards into your study schedule can really help you stay on track. Although the ultimate reward is getting a better grade and learning the material, you may find those goals too distant to help you on a nightly level. After all, everyone wants straight As (or at least straight Bs to keep your parents off your back), but that goal may not seem as relevant at 9 o'clock at night when you are really tired and have a trigonometry test the next day. Instead, try rewarding yourself with small, simple pleasures—for example, each night you cross off all the to-dos in your calendar, reward yourself by watching your favorite show or shooting hoops. Good grades and improvements in your learning and skills are rewards in and of themselves, but you should also be sure to reward yourself by taking time out once you've completed your work.

If your parents don't understand why you are taking time off to watch TV, be sure to show them your schedule and remind them that you are keeping up-to-date. Work out with them a consistent and reasonable reward schedule that allows you to get your work done but that also enables you to celebrate mini-steps along the way towards completing a large project such as studying for a test or writing a paper.

The Top 10 Obstacles to Studying and How to Defeat Them

Let's face it—there are a lot of good reasons NOT to study. Here are among the most popular reasons students never get around to doing their work, and you can probably think of several others. There is always a reason not to study, and the modern world has created a million alluring distractions in the form of cell phones, instant messaging, texting, the World Wide Web, video games, Facebook, MySpace, cable television, and satellite radio. However, there are ways around these obstacles—if you really want to find them. Here are some suggestions about how to avoid procrastination. In imitation of David Letterman, we'll count down the "Top 10 Obstacles to Studying" and discuss how to potentially overcome each obstacle.

10. You are distracted by computer games, Facebook, and other electronic amusements.

Some students find it necessary to completely unplug if they are going to get any work done. They disable the internet on their computer in order to avoid the temptation to IM and look at Facebook while they are trying to do homework. While this is an extreme measure, it's sometimes necessary. You can also try doing your work at school computers where there are no such applications and reserve home computers for fun and games.

9. You can't sit down.

Sitting down and getting started can be the hardest part of studying. Once you sit down and open the book, you can get going, but you may continue to procrastinate so that you eat into your study time. One trick to avoid continual procrastination is to have a "study buddy"—someone who works alongside you and forces you to study. Meet up with a reliable friend in the library or right after school, and make a pact with that person to get to your work right away. You don't even need to talk to the person—simply sitting at the same table can be an incentive for you to get started. Once you get started, you'll find that you keep rolling.

8. You don't have time.

Having insufficient time to study is a common complaint among students. If you find that you are constantly pressed for time, step back and analyze your week. You may want to even keep a log of how you spend each day. You may be surprised by how much time you spend watching television, texting your friends, or simply staring into space. After becoming more aware of how you spend your time, come up with a new schedule that eliminates these wasted times and that builds in defined relaxation times. For example, instead of staring into space while trying to study for math, schedule a 45-minute math study session, followed by 30 minutes watching television. You may need to write your schedule on a white board or a large piece of paper in your room to make sure you stick to it. You can also program devices such as pagers and PDAs to ring to remind you to get started on your studying.

If you find that you're not wasting time but simply don't have sufficient time, you should step back and analyze your schedule. Perhaps you need to cut back on the hours you work at an after-school job, if possible, or you may need to temporarily reduce the time you socialize with friends during the week to make sure you have time to dedicate to your work.

7. You hate the material.

No one likes studying boring material, or material that she finds totally uninteresting. It's unrealistic to expect that you are going to like everything you study in school. However, you might find that once you start studying the material, it becomes more interesting to you. Perhaps the reason you dislike it is that you simply don't understand it or that you feel distanced or uninterested in class. Once you get into the work, you may appreciate it more. You may also want to ask for help from your teacher or from a student in the class who seems to be enjoying it. Can this student explain to you why this subject is interesting to him or her? You may find there is something to like about what you are studying.

6. You hate the teacher.

You may click with some teachers and not with others. There is bound to be a teacher who seems confusing or even cruel to you, and you are entitled to your feelings about that teacher. However, you are not entitled to make your feelings about the teacher an excuse for not studying or caring about that class. It's your job to learn to learn from all kinds of teachers. If you think you are on the wrong side of the teacher, you may try to sit down with the teacher and figure out where you are going wrong. Sometimes, students annoy teachers without even realizing they are doing so. For example, your teacher may think you aren't working hard because you have mediocre grades and don't speak much in class. If you meet with this person, you can tell him that you are working hard and even show him your study guide or your class notes. Teachers like people who like their class, so be sure to show interest in the material and in doing well when you meet with the teacher, even if you have to manufacture your interest a bit. If the teacher likes you more, you may find that you like the class more as a result.

5. You aren't doing well in the class.

It's understandable not to like a class in which you aren't doing well. It's your job to figure out why you're not doing well. Simply believing, "I'm just not good at math or Spanish" or whatever class it is may not be accurate. Have you taken the time to ask your teacher's advice about how to study for tests and how to do well in the class? Perhaps the teacher can suggest a study method that's better suited to you and that you've overlooked. Be sure also to recognize small steps toward reaching your goal. Many students set unrealistically high expectations of themselves and then feel disappointed when they don't reach their goal. If you've been getting Ds in math and suddenly get a B, recognize this grade as a great achievement and as a step in the right direction. Reward yourself for achieving goals related to learning—not always related to grades. If you understand the material better after you meet with the teacher, recognize that your grades will improve over time—maybe just not right away.

4. You don't understand the material.

If you really don't understand the material when you sit down to study, you need to admit that and seek help where available. You can go to your parents, a trusted adult, a fellow student, the teacher, another teacher, or to a tutor for help. Admitting that you don't understand isn't the same as conceding defeat—instead, it's the first step toward removing an obstacle in your path and helping you to eventually succeed. Remember that even Einstein was thought stupid when he was a small child, perhaps because his teachers didn't quite understand what he had to offer. Very few people are naturals—most people need to work and work before they master something. If you are like 99.9% of humanity with regard to needing to ask for help, recognize your place in the human race and accept it.

3. You feel too pressured.

Often students procrastinate to blow off pressure. After all, if you don't deal with something, it won't bother you as much. How many times have you said to yourself, like Scarlett O'Hara in the famous movie *Gone with the Wind*, "I'll just think about that tomorrow" when you are faced with an unpleasant task or troubling reality? Procrastination can be the result of too much pressure—not too little. If you feel overly stressed, evaluate why you are feeling this way. Is it because you have unrealistic expectations, or because your parents expect you to achieve miracles? If you tend to be a perfectionist, you may not sit down to study because the first few passes at new material aren't about perfection—they are about getting better each time. You may not understand the material the first time you sit down to look at it, but that doesn't mean you will never understand it. Be sure to give yourself time to acquaint yourself with new material and time to make mistakes. After all, why do sports teams and professional athletes practice so much? It's because no one is perfect the first time around.

2. You have too much time.

Having too much time is more often a reason for procrastination and ineffective studying than having too little time. If you have too much time, you will most likely not feel pressured to study, and you will fritter away your time. Often, athletes find that they do better during their playing season because they have no time to waste and so they sit down to their work right when they get home. If you have too much free time, you need to structure your schedule—perhaps by adding constructive, energizing activities such as sports, drama, after-school clubs, exercise, or service activities. You can then feel more pressured to do your work during the time that remains to you. Obviously, you don't want to go overboard and overschedule your time, but a totally open calendar may not allow you to get enough done.

1. You don't see the point.

This is probably the hardest obstacle to defeat. If you don't see the point of studying algebraic expressions, you probably won't want to do so. It's the rare individual who can just study material because it's assigned, and studying out of fear of failing or simply for a grade is sometimes not very motivating. There's no easy answer to this problem. Perhaps if you ask your teacher to discuss the practical application of some of what you're studying, you'll see the point more directly. However, sometimes what you study in school is simply to introduce you to a discipline that you may or may not use later on and to develop what teachers like to call your "critical thinking skills." It may help you to simply see school as a kind of game. Perhaps it's not as fun as World of Warcraft or Grand Theft Auto, but it's nonetheless a game in which you can learn strategy and apply it to earn points. It might be more fun to you if you see some of what you study in this way.

CHECK-IN: What are your obstacles to studying?

Write down at least one potential strategy to overcome each of your obstacles.

_____

_____

_____

_____

_____

_____

_____

Chapter 3:
Playing and Winning the Testing "Game"

"Psyching Out" the Test—and Your Teacher

One of the most critical parts of preparing for tests is to understand the "game" of your class—not just the basic rules, but the parts of the game that no one teaches you directly. In baseball, for example, everyone knows that three outs end an inning. That's a basic, stated rule. However, it takes some time playing the game before you realize that a batter who has a runner on third will most likely hit to first base so the runner can score. Even video games have unwritten rules—strategies you know will help you because you've played the game before.

Understanding the unwritten rules of a test mean reading between the lines to determine what the teacher thinks is important and how the teacher wants you to answer specific types of questions. ***It's vital to know all the rules of a class, even if some aren't directly stated.*** Just as you have to know the written and unwritten rules before you start playing a video game, knowing the rules before you go into a test is critical. In fact, school is very similar to a video game: there are two main players—you and your teacher--and you have to rack up points before the game is over.

However, unlike a video game, school doesn't have a "re-start button." Many students would like to push the re-start button when they don't do well on a test or when they get on the wrong side of a teacher. Unfortunately, school doesn't come with a restart button—so you have to play wisely and well from the beginning.

The first rule of the "school game" to remember is that whether you like it or not, your teacher is the one counting your points—not you. And at the end of the game, your teacher is going to tell you if you won—or lost. You may think your teacher is as merciless as Simon on *American Idol* or as wise as Harry Potter's Albus Dumbledore. You are welcome to think whatever you want of your teacher, but remember that he or she will decide your grade, and you have to do what you can to get your teacher interested in your well-being. Yes, there is a "fuzzy" part of grading, and if your teacher likes you, you will most likely do better. That doesn't mean you will automatically get an A, but it might mean the difference between a C+ and a B- or the difference between a B+ and A-.

That brings us to how to understand what is going to be on your test. Believe or not, there are often ways to tell what the teacher is going to ask you before you head into a test—even if he or she doesn't tell you directly or give you a review sheet or a list of topics. Perhaps you haven't been paying attention to what the teacher thinks is important. You may find a class so dull that you tend to zone out. Simply put, don't. Teachers will often give you cues that alert you to what they are going to ask, and tuning into their signals is part of successful test-taking.

Tip #1: Pay attention to what interests the teacher

Pay attention to what the teacher spends a lot of time on and what he or she seems interested in on the days leading up to a test. For example, do the teachers' eyes light up when he talks about Plato in a unit on Ancient Greece? Odds are that he will ask you about his favorite subject matter. To be a good student, you have to put yourself in the shoes of your teachers (no matter how ugly and unfashionable your teachers' footwear is). Teachers have to grade a lot of tests, so they'd much rather ask you questions about the subjects in their course that interest them the most.

Many students struggle to figure out what the teacher will ask them, but by watching your teacher and figuring out what he or she spends a lot of time on, you will develop a natural method of psyching out the test. In addition, you will only increase your teachers' fondness for you if you at least fake an intense interest in what they like. Even if you hate math and don't understand why on earth you should study it, don't voice such opinions aloud to your teacher. Recall that he has spent his life learning and teaching math, and such comments will only wind up hurting your chances of getting him to like you. After all, if he insulted something you were interested in—whether it was snowboarding or the playlist on your iPod—you wouldn't be pleased.

Tip #2: Ask your teacher for what you need for testing.

There are some areas over which students may not have control. For example, if you have problems concentrating and tend to be disorganized, you may find it hard to sit still, and you may fidget in class and need to get up for frequent bathroom breaks. You may forget your homework on occasion, and you have to accept that occasionally, such events are going to happen and that you can't push that magical "re-start button," as you can while playing video games. If your teacher likes you and thinks you are working hard and are interested in the class, the teacher might look the other way at some of your foibles or little mistakes. If, on the other hand, you have spent most of your time ripping apart sheets of paper and building fake mounds of snow with it on your desk, the teacher is likely to crack down on you and not forgive some of the behaviors you may find it hard to control.

If you are in the good graces of your teacher, your tests will also most likely go better. For example, you may need to get up to take a break during a test, and if a teacher understands you are working hard, he or she will be more likely to allow you to take breaks, or to get up and walk around during a test. You may also need the following kinds of accommodations or help on a test:

- the ability to break up tests and take them over a longer period
- having the teacher read your test questions out loud so you understand them
- using graph paper for math tests so you can align your columns
- using a computer for writing on tests
- using a calculator during math tests
- getting permission to walk around during tests
- taking tests in a quiet room apart from other students and noise

For more information, please see the later chapter on "Getting and Using Accommodations."

Check-in: Do you need to ask your teacher for any of these accommodations?_____

If so, please see the later chapter on accommodations.

Real-life Strategy: Emma spent most of the first quarter of her eighth grade year alienating her Algebra teacher. She joked around in class, used her laptop to view her Facebook page, and repeatedly told poor Mr. McDonald—who had taught middle school math for 25 years—that math was useless and stupid. She never went to see him for extra help outside of class, though she found that she didn't really understand the material. After receiving a "C" for the first quarter, she quickly changed her attitude. She had never received a grade below a "B" in math before, and she knew that although it had always come easy to her, the material had become too difficult for her to stop paying attention.

Emma realized that she had to work differently. She knew that because of her "receptive-language" issue, she didn't always pick up all the information in class. She needed to meet with Mr. McDonald once a week during her lunch period. She also found that she could concentrate better during these one-on-one sessions. To prepare for her meetings with her teacher, she tried to pay more attention in class by moving her seat away from her friends, who goofed around. She went to Mr. McDonald with specific questions from the homework that she didn't understand. She also got a copy of the math notes from a friend who took good notes in class. Using these strategies, she pulled her grade up to a "B" in the second quarter.

Tip #3: Learn how to speak your teacher's language.

Part of getting what you need for testing is of course learning to ask for it. Once a teacher likes you, you will feel more comfortable asking for breaks during tests or for extra copies of the review sheets you've lost. But what if you don't know your teacher or trust her, and you have to ask her for permission to take breaks or to sit in the front row? You may feel uncomfortable about asking for these types of accommodations, and yet they may be vital to allowing you to pay attention in class and to doing well on tests.

The key to asking for what you need from teachers is to speak their language. In class, you may have wished that teachers learned to speak your language. Teachers say things like, "a function is an equation in which an x will yield exactly one y." That's math teacher talk, but it doesn't mean it makes a bit of sense to you. You may have asked yourself, "why don't math teachers simply say, 'you put a number into this equation and get out another number. The number you put in is x, and for reasons we cannot possibly reveal to you—or we'd have to kill you—the number you get out is y.'"?

In the same way, teachers often wish you would speak THEIR language. When you ask for what you need from teachers, be sure to consider your requests in terms of what the teachers think is important. For example, you may ask a teacher to sit in the front row by saying, "I know you have to move around the assigned seating, but it would really help me to concentrate, particularly in light of the upcoming test, if I sat in the front row. I've been working really hard on my homework, and sitting in the front row will allow me to concentrate during the review." Or, you could say something like, "Mr. Dumbledore, I'm wondering if you'd have time to meet before our next math test to review multiplying fractions. I can meet you right after school—if you're free. I've gone over my homework problems, and I have only two to ask you about."

Notice in these examples that you ask clearly for what you need but you also show the teacher that you've been working hard, that you have specific questions to ask the teacher (so you won't waste time with complaining or simply saying, "I don't get it!"), and that you want to do well. You also have to acknowledge that changes such as moving your seat or requests such as meeting with the teacher may cause extra work for them. The best gift you can give your teacher is your interest in doing well in the class, so be sure to emphasize that what you are asking for will help you improve your understanding and your grade.

Tip #4: Clarify directions with your teacher.

The importance of this tip can not be overestimated. So many students go astray when they don't clarify what their teacher is looking for—on papers, tests, and other assignments. While you shouldn't constantly pester your teacher, you should be sure you are on the right track when tackling a major assignment. Even if your teacher explains the assignment in class, you may not be paying attention to everything the teacher says. Be sure to read the assignment sheets teachers give you quite carefully. Many students lose points by not reading the fine print of assignments (Examples: "Do not use Wikipedia for this research paper." Or, "use at least three sources." Or, "Start your essay exam with a strong thesis statement and support it with **three** examples.") When you read the assignment sheet, take out a highlighter and underline key words such as "three examples" or key deadlines. Then, be sure to transfer these deadlines into your assignment book and work backwards to plan out exactly how you are going to accomplish all the small steps to getting your work completed.

In addition to reading assignment sheets carefully, be sure to read directions on tests carefully. Many students get test questions wrong because they read the directions incorrectly. You may even want to underline key parts of directions such as, "Each of the following is an example of a Tudor king EXCEPT…." Underlining key words will force you to slow down and read questions correctly, sparing you from knowing the information but still getting the questions wrong. If you feel that you don't understand directions during a test, be sure to clarify them with your teacher. While your teacher can't give you answers on tests, he or she can clarify what the test asks for and if you are answering in the right way.

Maintaining Focus and Concentration While Studying

You may find it difficult to study for a test because your mind wanders. If you have an iPod, Wii, and Tivo nearby, your task may be nearly impossible. You may decide to play one game of Wii tennis, and, five hours later, find that you haven't done a lick of work. If your computer has IMing, you may spend what seems like just a few minutes chatting with your friends and going on Facebook before you find that it's midnight and you haven't even read one page in your history textbook for the test you have tomorrow. The strategies below will help you concentrate better in a world filled with addictive distractions.

Tip #1: Unplug.

Yes, it may be difficult—nearly impossible—but you must pull the plug on your Wii, your Internet, your PS2, and whatever fun devices you have around. Yes, these devices have made life a lot more fun— but they've also made school seem ten times duller than even in your parents' day. Back in the day—meaning the 1980s, of course—MTV was new, there were no iPods, and the Internet had yet be invented for popular use. Therefore, schoolwork didn't seem half as dull as today. Atari was fun, but the graphics weren't one quarter as good as those on World of Warcraft. This is all to say that the creative minds working on video games have made them so much fun that they can be totally and utterly addictive. To compensate and save your academic life, you must at times unplug. That means remove the Internet from your computer. Disable the IM function entirely. Pretends it's 1974 and HDTV doesn't exist. If you know that you can't study without constantly checking Facebook, you are left with no other choice than to go completely wireless.

Often, students will find it easier to concentrate with some music playing, and music is fine as long as it doesn't interfere with your studying. Low background music can help some students concentrate better because it gives their minds a kind of activity that combats restlessness and that relaxes them.

Check-in: Do you need to unplug yourself? _____

If so, how will you do so? _____

_____

_____

_____

_____

Do you need a trusted person, such as a parent or friend, to help you enforce your new rules about studying? If so, whom will you ask?

_____

Tip #2: Engage in frequent, short periods of misery.

Break up your studying into short, frequent sessions. For example, if you have a biology test coming up on Thursday, spend Sunday afternoon studying the digestive tract from the tongue through the stomach and use Wednesday afternoon to review and go from the stomach to the small intestine and onward. Don't try to cram everything into your head at once—you will stress yourself out, and you won't be able to retain the information as well as if you study for short periods of time. Speaking of the digestive system, studying is like eating a meal with many courses. You want to eat the soup first, then give yourself time before downing the salad, pause before the main course, and then wait a while before dessert. Everything goes down more smoothly when your stomach has time to process each course—just as everything gets into your brain more coherently when you give yourself time to digest the information.

It's fine to snack (or digest small amounts of material) in between meals. In other words, find little pockets of time to study—such as when you're on the bus or doing sit-ups while watching *Lost*. While you shouldn't do serious studying while watching TV, you can spend fifteen minutes reviewing your flashcards on the Civil War generals or on Spanish verbs—as long as it's simply review.

Tip #3: Reward yourself as if you were a dog.

Have you ever trained a dog or watched a dog show? If so, you've noted that after each trick, the dog is given a treat—often out of the trainer's mouth! Canine principles apply to people, too. After each study session in which you've worked hard, try to find time to do something that revives you or rewards you. For example, if it's 7 o'clock and you know that your favorite show is on at 9, try to finish studying by then so you can watch an hour of TV as a reward. In addition, using bookends such as going out with friends or watching TV will help motivate you to finish your studying in a timely way. If your BFFs (best friends forever, of course) are meeting for Frappuccinos at Starbuck's at 7 and it's now 5, knowing that you only have two hours to finish your work might help you push yourself to start.

Having too much time to study is can pose its own problems. Many students find that they procrastinate until they have to do something. For more tips on time-management strategies and how to stop procrastinating, see Chapter 2.

Check-in: How will you reward yourself for studying?

_____

_____

_____

_____

_____

Tip #4: Try to find a creative way to approach problems.

For example, one student made a game out of shuffling and reshuffling her Latin vocabulary flash cards. Although she still would rather watch TV than study, she found that she was motivated to study vocabulary by making a game out of throwing down cards and seeing if she knew the definitions of the words. By using this strategy, she improved her vocabulary for an upcoming test in a few short periods of studying. Use your own intelligence and creativity to come out with strategies and games that will motivate you to study.

Check-in: Think of a creative strategy to study for your upcoming test.

_____

_____

_____

_____

Tip #5: Use your favorite learning strategy.

Try to use your favorite way of studying that you discovered in the first chapter on "Shopping for a Learning Style." For example, if you are primarily an auditory learner, you may find that your attention drifts when you are reading a book to study for a test. Try listening to your textbook on tape (available through Recordings for the Blind and Dyslexic; see "Helpful Books and Websites") or recording what you need to know onto an iPod. Using your favorite type of strategy will help you maintain your focus.

Tip #6: Study after exercising.

Exercise makes the brain more receptive to new information, and running around the block relaxes the body and curbs restlessness. In addition, exercise releases feel-good chemicals in the brain that make studying seem less burdensome. Obviously, you don't want to be totally worn out by the time you hit the books, but a vigorous twenty-minute walk can make you more attentive and relaxed.

Real-life Strategy: When Brian, a student with ADD, entered a competitive public high school in 9th grade, he found that he simply wasn't able to concentrate long enough on his loads of nightly reading. While he had done well enough in middle school, the amount of reading he received in high school was much greater. He decided to ask his doctor for a short-lasting ADD medication that he could take after school that would enable him to concentrate without interfering with his sleep. He also found that he concentrated well after taking a half-hour jog before settling down to his work. Exercise cleared his mind of the stress of the day, helped him feel focused and calm, and kept him in shape.

A Note on Medication

If you have been prescribed medication for ADD such as Ritalin or Concerta by a doctor, you should take the exact dose that he or she recommended. Students who haven't been diagnosed with a condition that requires medication sometimes think that taking medication for ADD will help them. There has never been any evidence that this is true, and, aside from the illegality of buying and using prescription drugs that aren't yours, you should be wary of taking medication whose effect is unknown to you. On the day of an important test, you want to feel rested and confident—not "weirded out" and confused by the effects of an unfamiliar drug. Taking illegal medication is **not** the way to do well on a test, and despite urban legends and stories that go around that this medication helps you, the most important strengths you bring to the test are your confidence and knowledge of the test and what it covers. You can't take a pill that makes you understand the material better.

Tip #1: Work with your doctor to find the right dose and the right schedule for tests and studying.

If you like to take days off from taking your medication, work with your doctor to determine when you definitely need to take your medication. The day of a test or the day you need to spend studying for a test are likely **not** the best times to take a vacation from your medication. As you consult with your doctor on an on-going basis, be honest about what your schedule is like and when you need intensified periods of concentration.

Work with your doctor to find the dose of medication that will help you study. If you take medication in the morning, it may wear off by the time you need to do your homework or study for tests. Be sure to find the right does that will help you concentrate while studying without making you too wired to sleep. Your doctor may have you keep track of your schedule during the school week so you know when you need to take longer- or shorter-lasting medication so you can concentrate during school and after school for sports, after-school activities, or studying—while still being able to eat well and get the right amount of sleep. The most crucial step is to make sure you let your doctor know if your medication isn't working or if you are experiencing side effects such as insomnia, depression, or weight loss. **If you have any concerns, consult your doctor immediately.**

Check-in: Write here any issues about your medication that you want to remember to bring up with your doctor.

_____

_____

_____

_____

_____

How to Calm Down and Not Rush

You may find that you feel incredibly pressed for time while taking a test. In addition, you may feel so nervous that your palms are sweating and you feel faint. These are common reactions to tests—and many students have them. Years after graduating from high school, students have nightmares about erasing so much on 6th grade science tests that the paper rips. It's understandable that you are nervous, and a little bit of anxiety gets the brain moving.

However, you may find that you are so anxious that you can't concentrate and that you are rushing through problems on which you should take your time. As a result, you may make careless errors even if you know the material. Here are some strategies to help you avoid the jitters and take the time you need.

Tip #1: Build breathing into your technique.

Before you even get the test, practice breathing deeply and imaging the stress flowing out of your body. While this technique sounds like a time-waster, it has actually been shown that by simply concentrating on your breath and the tension in your back, you can relax. Don't spend the moments right before the test trying to cram in information; cramming doesn't work. Instead, take a minute to listen to an inspirational song on your iPod or to simply breathe deeply many times. Remember Olympic gold medalist Michael Phelps? Before each event, he put on his earphones and listened to music. This technique paid off for him in the Olympics, so it may also result in academic gold for you.

Tip #2: Find ways to slow down during the test.

While taking the test, it's of course hard to practice deep breathing. There are other techniques you can use to make sure you aren't rushing. For example, you can put your pencil down after each math problem or after each short-answer section in a history or English test. You can glance out the window for ten seconds to catch a relaxing glimpse of the blue sky and then turn back to your work.

Check-in: Brainstorm some ideas about how to slow yourself down appropriately during tests so that you're not rushing but so that you don't run out of time, either.

_____

_____

_____

_____

_____

_____

Tip #3: Use your pencil to highlight and cross out.

Have you ever misread questions on a test so you answered the wrong way? To avoid this mistake, underline the question. While this strategy seems very simple, it will force you to slow down and to read the question carefully. Slow down enough to ask yourself what exactly the question is asking for. If there are different parts to the question, be sure to note them and answer each part. For multiple-choice questions, you can underline or even double-underline words such as "EXCEPT" so that you pay extra close attention to this part of the question. Cross out incorrect answer choices on multiple-choice questions so that you can concentrate on the answer choices that remain.

On math tests, you can use a highlighter to highlight signs, such as + or -. Using a bright highlighter pen will force you to pay attention to the signs and help you avoid making careless mistakes.

During long tests such as standardized tests, stretch during breaks and eat energy-sustaining snacks such as yogurt and fruit and power bars instead of candy bars and cookies. Take advantage of any breaks you have to get up and walk around. If you don't have a break given by the teacher, you can excuse yourself to go to the bathroom or get a drink. While you don't want to waste too much time, these short one- to two-minute breaks can really help you curb your restlessness and maintain your focus when you get back to the test.

A Note on Bubbling in Answers

Some students have experienced the worst nightmare on standardized tests or other kinds of tests that require you to fill in "bubbles" or circles with the right answer choice—they knew a lot of the right answers but their bubbling was off. That is, they filled in the wrong bubbles or got off track by one question when filling in answers. Be sure to "subvocalize"—that is, speak under you breath—each time you bubble in an answer. Say to yourself, "this is question one, and I'm bubbling in the answer for line 1." It may seem simplistic, but this technique helps you stay on track and get the score you deserve.

Is there Any Way to Enjoy Studying?

You may be thinking to yourself, "some people enjoy living in isolated ice caves, but that doesn't mean I have to." Tests may seem to you like one of the Biblical plagues sent to earth to torment poor mortals and exhaust them so that they're too tired to act out much in school. Yes, there is truth to that—few people like studying or taking tests, but is there a way to find a silver lining in the midst of the cloud of test-taking? It's sort of like thinking about the lollipop or new toothbrush you get after going to the dentist or orthodontist.

Tip #1: Make studying and test-taking into a game.

If you like playing basketball or another sport, you can apply the same kinds of strategies to taking tests. Remember—your goal is come up with a strategy to get more points. Analyze your previous tests the way you would your performance on the court. What did you do right? What did you do wrong? How can you get some easy points here or there? How can you psych out the enemy—in this case, the test—the next time around? Teachers give so many tests that you will always have a new opportunity to take on your archrival and do better the next time around.

Be sure to celebrate your victories and learn from your losses. After you've done well on a test, analyze what you did right. Did you break up your studying and do a bit of work over several nights? Did you use your preferred study technique that you found in the first chapter? Did you see your teacher before the test? Did you get notes from a friend if you missed school? These strategies are all part of your training, and you should be sure to apply them the next time you take a test. If you didn't do as well as you had wanted, be sure to analyze what you could do better the next time around. Be sure to check out the last chapter on using your results to improve. Remember—there is no such thing as a really bad test score in the long run, as long as you use your score to improve.

Check-in: What did you do right before the last test? Was there anything you did wrong, and, if so, what will you do differently next time?

_____

_____

_____

_____

_____

_____

Tip #2: Remember that you have an excuse to reward yourself.

If you break up your studying over time and study a little bit for an upcoming test over several nights, you have an automatic excuse to feel good about yourself and of course reward yourself accordingly. You may have tended to put off studying by guiltily watching TV, talking on the phone, IMing, cleaning lint out of the fan in your bathroom, Googling your neighbors, shooting baskets with crumpled-up papers, unfolding paperclips, doodling, and analyzing the downfall of Britney Spears. While these activities are no doubt worthwhile, you may not realize that you will have a lot more fun by doing your work for a limited period of time—say, a good half hour—and then taking a much-deserved break when you can do something really fun without feeling guilty. If you break up your studying, you can build in fun rewards such as watching your favorite TV show without feeling any remorse.

Tip #3: Take advantage of fun projects.

Occasionally—though it may seem rare—your teacher will give you some material that you are actually interested in! For example, you may be able to write a research paper on something that interests you—such as a book you like or a research paper on Jackie Robinson or the rise of professional theater. Some teachers give you the option to do a poster or write a song in place of some tests. Take the opportunity and use it for all it's worth. While these types of assignments may not be as enjoyable as actually playing baseball or acting in a play, they are still better than taking a regular test—so take advantage of them to allow your talents and interests to shine.

Tip #4: Try to see a connection between schoolwork and you.

While a lot of what you study in school seems pointless and boring, there are times when you can connect what's going on in the classroom to your life. For example, if you are studying a language, try to go to a restaurant where the staff speak that language so you can practice, possibly feel foolish, and understand that there is a connection between your life and what you are learning. If you are studying interest rates in math, try to use what you've learned to re-organize your bank accounts or your saving techniques. If you are studying the Industrial Revolution, look for the connection to cars, your iBook, or 747s. The information might seem slightly less useless, and you might find yourself a bit more motivated to study it.

Chapter 4:
Becoming Jane Austen: Acing Essay Tests

Preparing for Essay Tests

Preparing for an essay test is critical. If your English or history teacher gives you the topic or an idea of the topic of the essay beforehand, much of your work can be finished before you even step into the classroom.

You can prepare for the typical five-paragraph essay test by using the following template:

ESSAY TEMPLATE

Paragraph 1: Introduction
- Write two to three sentences about the background of your essay. Let the reader of the essay know the main ideas that you will cover.
- Write a thesis statement that contains the claim you will prove in your essay. Typically, the thesis is the last sentence in the first paragraph.

Paragraph 2: The first body paragraph
- Write a transition sentence that moves from the thesis to the point of the first body paragraph.
- Introduce your first example. If this example is a quote from a book, be sure to include the quote within quotation marks ("). After using the example, be sure to discuss it.
- Be sure that your example(s) support the claim that you established in the thesis statement in the introductory paragraph.

Paragraph 3: The second body paragraph
- Follow the directions for the first body paragraph, using your second example, quote, or claim.

Paragraph 4: The third body paragraph
- Follow the directions for the first body paragraph, using your third and final example, quote, or claim.

Paragraph 5: Conclusion
- Restate your thesis in different words.
- Write a conclusion that shows why your point is important. This is perhaps the hardest part of the essay because you have to connect what you are writing to a larger point. We will discuss the conclusion in greater depth in the sample essay that follows.

This template is appropriate for the type of essay that establishes a claim and then tries to prove the claim. The thesis statement is really the claim you are making, and the middle three paragraphs provide support (one idea in each paragraph) for your claim. Writing an essay is kind of like being a lawyer in court. For example, you set out to prove a claim such as, "My client is innocent." Then, you provide at least three reasons why your client is innocent and discuss each claim. You summarize your evidence in your conclusion and re-state your claim. Your reader is like the jury. He or she decides if you've proven your claim by supporting it with solid evidence. ***So, you want your essay to be clear, well-supported, and well-organized.***

Here is a sample essay on a very simplistic and somewhat silly topic. Keep in mind that the organizations and statistics in the essay are entirely fictitious (although it is of course important to start your day with food). However, it will allow you to see how to use each of the elements in the essay template above. Each element is noted in parentheses before the element is used in the essay.

SAMPLE ESSAY:
WHY AMERICAN TEENAGERS SHOULD EAT BREAKFAST

INTRODUCTION: (Background) Breakfast is perhaps the most underappreciated meal in the United States today. Data gathered by the U.S. Federation of Concerned Parents show that 85% of American teenagers do not eat breakfast regularly. However, teenagers skip the first meal of the day at their own peril. **(Thesis)** <u>Breakfast has been shown to improve students' energy levels, improve their grades, and facilitate their communication with parents and teachers.</u>

(Transition sentence) While most students skip breakfast in favor of later gorging themselves with french fries and other fatty food at lunch, teenagers would have more energy if they started off the day with a nutritious meal. **(SUPPORT #1)** In a recent study conducted by the U.S. Department of Teenager Energy, students aged 14-18 who had wholegrain cereal and oranges for breakfast were able to run an average of 5 times around a one-mile track. A similar set of teenagers who had skipped breakfast ran an average of only once around this same track. **(ANALYSIS OF SUPPORT)** This study shows clearly that those teenagers who eat whole grains and fruit when they get up are better able to handle physical and other demands with greater energy than those students who haven't eaten in the morning.

(Transition sentence connecting first support to second) In addition to boosting energy levels, eating breakfast helps students perform better at mental tasks at school. **(SUPPORT #2)** At Glenview High School, a poll in last year's newspaper showed that 90% of students on the honor roll regularly ate breakfast, while only 50% of other students did so. Says straight-A student Harvey Pookah, "Before I ate breakfast every day—and I mean a complete meal with cereal, cranberry juice, pears, and sometimes kiwis—I was totally unable to concentrate during chemistry class. However, since I started eating this fruit-laden meal each morning, I find chemistry riveting, and I'm doing much better on pop quizzes." **(ANALYZE SUPPORT)** This study and Mr. Pookah's experience show the beneficial mental effects of eating breakfast.

(Transition sentence connecting third body paragraph to earlier paragraphs). Breakfast not only boosts students' mental and physical energy, it also helps students get along better with their elders. **(SUPPORT #3)**. According to Dr. Nora McStudy, teenagers who find their parents and teachers extremely irritating on a regular level can be helped by a simple bowl of non-sugar cereal. Says Dr. McStudy, "In my family medicine practice, I have seen dozens of teenagers for whom the simple addition of a balanced meal at the beginning of the day lessens school and familial tension." Adds junior Clara Devlin, "Before I ate breakfast, I thought my mother looked like a moose, and I told her so. However, after some whole-wheat toast, I found I was much better able to put up with her." **(ANALYSIS OF EVIDENCE)** Therefore, the cutting-edge work of Dr. McStudy shows that a simple meal in the morning can help teenagers get along better with the adults they are forced to contend with on a daily level.

(CONCLUSION) The benefits of breakfast are manifold and include better energy, increased mental edge, and improved relations with adults. **(WIDER POINT)** Students who do not eat breakfast are doing themselves a great disservice. With the addition of a simple meal in the morning, teenagers may find their lives easier to manage, and national student productivity may increase as a result.

Notice in this essay that the thesis statement is underlined. There are three main points introduced in the first paragraph: eating breakfast improves physical energy, increases mental energy, and improves teenagers' relationships with teachers and parents. Each body paragraph is devoted to supporting ONE of these ideas in greater detail, and the concluding paragraph summarizes the information and notes its larger importance.

PRACTICE: Use this template to prepare for an in-class writing essay or a take-home piece of writing. How did the template help you? What parts of the essay did you find difficult? If you need to hone your practice, write down the elements you need to work on below:

_____

_____

_____

_____

_____

_____

_____

_____

_____

_____

_____

_____

_____

_____

_____

_____

_____

_____

_____

_____

_____

The Advantages of Preparing an Essay Beforehand

The template and sample essay above give you an idea of how to structure an essay. While the essays you write will be more complicated in terms of their content, you can use this template to write most essays, depending on the demands of your teacher. If your teacher is agreeable to looking at rough drafts of an essay before the test or in-class writing exercise, you can show him or her your outline and see what corrections the teacher makes. In addition, some teachers allow students to bring index cards or a sheet of paper with a thesis statement and evidence to the test. If your teacher allows this kind of preparation, you should of course take advantage of this opportunity and come to the essay test with your outline fully prepared. Some teachers also allow you to bring in the book on which you have to write your essay. If so, you should find each of the quotes you plan to use ahead of time and mark them in your book with a Post-it note for easy reference. Be sure to think ahead of time about how you will analyze each quote and about your thesis statement and conclusion. Again, run your thoughts by your teacher.

After Writing: Attending to Grammar, Handwriting, and Organization

After you write your essay, go back and make sure the grammar is correct. Some students have a hard time seeing their mistakes and correcting them. If you feel unsure about grammar, be sure to note the mistakes that your teacher corrects on your tests. You may want to write down your mistakes in a special notebook and review them so that you are sure not to repeat them. If you need a review of grammar, use Diana Hacker's *A Writer's Reference* (see "Helpful Books and Websites"). This book will acquaint you with some of the common grammatical mistakes many students make and show you how to fix them.

Many students find it difficult to write by hand because they are used to writing on a computer. Some schools allow students to use laptops to take essay tests, but most do not. Therefore, you may have to get used to writing by hand, even if you have messy handwriting. Teachers are usually experts at handwriting analysis, as many students' handwriting styles resemble Egyptian hieroglyphics. However, you want to make your handwriting as legible as possible by writing in capital letters if necessary, by making your letters large enough, and by skipping lines if needed.

After writing, you also want to review the organization of your essay. Check that your evidence relates back to your thesis. In addition, make sure that your conclusion is connected to your thesis. Check over the flow of ideas, and ask yourself if you've written good transition sentences that connect the new idea in each body paragraph to what has come before in the essay.

Real-life strategy: Nick was a good writer who had interesting ideas about the novels he read in his 9th grade English class. However, he received a poor grade on an in-class essay he wrote on "The Great Gatsby" by F. Scott Fitzgerald because his ideas were totally unorganized. Nick had ADD, and he found it difficult to organize everything he wanted to say in the pressured in-class writing period. However, his tutor showed him how to follow a template, or a set of rules, for each essay. By following this template and using it for each essay test, Nick found that he was able to produce well-organized essays that expressed his insightful ideas in a clear, organized manner.

Below is a check-list that you should use after you've written an essay to make sure that you've accomplished what you set out to do:

ESSAY WRITING CHECK-LIST

- **Did I write a strong thesis statement that summarizes my argument?**
- **Did I write transition sentences at the beginning of each body paragraph connecting the new material to what came before?**
- **Did I include sufficient support to prove my points?**
- **Did I analyze my evidence after I introduced it?**
- **Does my conclusion relate back to my thesis statement?**
- **Did I end with a strong statement that connects what I wrote to a broader, more important point?**
- **Did I review my essay for grammar, spelling mistakes, handwriting, and other errors?**

Improving Your Vocabulary

An important part of writing on essay tests is to have the right words at your disposal. Some students feel slowed down in writing because they don't have enough vocabulary at their fingertips. When writing at home, students tend to use the "synonyms" application in MS Word to find the correct word.

However, this tool can lead you to choose the wrong word because you don't understand the complete meaning of the word. In addition, this tool may not enable you to build your vocabulary over time. If you want to write good essays, you need to have an extensive vocabulary that you use correctly. Having a large vocabulary allows you to express your ideas precisely and without repetition.

As you read for school and outside of school, you should write down any words you don't know and then look up and write down their meanings. This practice will systematically help you improve your vocabulary over time. Although you most likely have to learn vocabulary for school, looking up words you encounter in books helps you understand the meaning of words in the context of longer passages and introduces you to an even wider array of words.

Here are some additional books you can use to build your vocabulary:

- ***Vocabulary Cartoons: Building an Educated Vocabulary With Visual Mnemonics*** by Sam Burchers, Max Burchers, and Bryan Burchers: This book is especially good for **visual learners**, as it provides a cartoon for each new word you learn.

- ***Picture These SAT Words in a Flash*** (**500 cards**) by Philip Geer. These vocabulary flash cards cover words on the SAT and words you may often encounter in high school. Visual learners can flip through the cards, auditory learners can use them to construct a tune, and kinesthetic learners can use the cards to play games.

- ***Shortcut to Word Power: Essential Latin and Greek Roots and Prefixes*** by Allan Sack. This book allows you to systematically use Latin and Greek roots and prefixes (the beginnings of words) to build your vocabulary. It's amazing how extensively you can build your "word power," as the authors call it, by knowing a few classical roots.

Real-life strategy: Julia had an expressive language disorder, which meant that she often struggled to write. She had good ideas, but she found that she simply couldn't express them well in writing. She couldn't find the right words to state her ideas. To improve her writing, she concentrated on using her Latin studies to understand the roots of English words. She learned the meanings of approximately twenty roots and prefixes that come from Latin and Greek and that are often used in English words. By doing so, she found that she was able to figure out the meanings of new English words and that she had increased her vocabulary. Having these words in her vocabulary allowed her to read material more quickly and to express herself better in writing.

CHECK-IN: How can you build your vocabulary? Write down two methods below.

_____

_____

Pacing

One of the most difficult elements of writing an essay is doing it within the time limit. Many students find that they run out of time on in-class writing exercises because they don't pace themselves appropriately. When you first receive the essay question in class, be sure to write down a very quick outline that takes about a few minutes. For example, if your question is why North won the Civil War, you would write something like the following:

- Thesis: North won because of superior manpower, despite weak military leaders.
- First paragraph: Weak military leaders in the North until U.S. Grant
  - McClellan: failed Peninsular campaign
- Second paragraph: North had more ships, industry, soldiers
- Third paragraph: South had better generals but less industry
  - importance of Jeff Davis
  - fewer soldiers, no slaves in Confederate army
- Conclusion: Superior manpower allowed North to win over time.

This kind of outline isn't as complete as the full essay template outlined above. However, it will enable you to preview all the ideas you want to cover in your essay. As the period for writing goes on, you want to pace yourself and give yourself a few minutes for each paragraph. Knowing the complete road map of your essay will allow you to cover all the material in a timely way to avoid covering material that is outside the scope of your essay. Be sure to also allow yourself a few minutes at the end of the test to review your work to make sure you have covered your outline and to review your grammar and organization.

Chapter 5:
Einstein Made Easy: Outwitting Math Tests

Taking a math test can be a lot like going to Paris. I don't mean to say that taking math tests is similar to having a delightful vacation enjoying chocolate croissants, marveling at the Eiffel Tower, and smelling fresh flowers. No, I mean that taking math tests can be like traveling a foreign country where you don't speak the language, the trains aren't running, and a poodle pees on your luggage. Some students would rather be hung by their toenails than take a math test—and with good reason. All those foreign symbols—xs, ys, derivatives, exponents, absolute values—it's almost as though math teachers don't speak our language. In fact, taking a math test make you feel as though you left your secret decoder ring at home, or like you never had one to begin with.

Part of your job in studying for math tests is to get to know the material so well that you can put it in your own words. Here are some strategies to help you avoid feeling that as you take math tests, you're trapped in a nightmare, a foreign vacation gone wrong, or a CIA mission in which you left your decoder ring in your dresser drawer.

First, analyze what may be getting in your way on math tests by using the checklist below. Then, find strategies for your specific obstacle.

CHECKLIST OF POTENTIAL MATH PITFALLS:
place a check beside each statement that applies to you:

_____ I tend to make careless computational errors on math tests. (If so, see "Avoiding Careless Mistakes.")

_____ I think I understand the material, but then I'm often fooled by different kinds of problems my teacher puts on a test (See "Studying for Math Tests.")

_____ I often do the wrong operation, such as subtracting rater than adding, because I read the problems incorrectly (See "Avoiding Careless Mistakes.")

_____ I often rush on math tests (See "Avoiding Rushing.")

_____ I have bad handwriting so I tend to mess up my columns and add, subtract, multiply, or divide incorrectly (See tip #2 under "Avoiding Careless Mistakes.")

_____ I tend to lose my place in long math problems that have many steps (See tip #3 under "Avoiding Careless Mistakes.")

_____ When I get a math test, I feel so panicked that it's like everything I know rushes out of my head (see "Dealing with Math Anxiety")

_____ I often give the wrong answer on word problems because I don't remember what the question is asking for (See "Avoiding Careless Mistakes.")

_____ I have a terrible memory for formulas and rules that I'm supposed to know on math tests (see tip #4 in "Avoiding Careless Mistakes")

Studying for Math Tests

Some students consider studying for math tests pointless. They often say, "either you know it or you don't." Apparently, some people also jump out of airplanes without checking that their parachutes work, but I wouldn't want to be one such person—would you?

Yes, maybe one-fifth of people can get math without studying, but, if my math is right, that leaves 5/4 (just kidding—I mean, 4/5) of people who don't get it right away. *Most people need to review for math tests—and here's why*. Although your teacher may give you review problems, remember that the problems on the test will be different. These are math teachers we're talking about. They delight in giving students surprise problems. They change numbers, flip figures around, and throw difficult loops into word problems and enjoy watching the rest of us math-illiterates squirm in our seats. That brings us to our first important strategy:

Tip #1: Understand concepts—don't just do review problems.

This is the number-one mistake of math students: they simply do the review sheets or re-do select problems from their math textbooks and wonder why they don't do well on tests. The answer is that shifty math-teacher behavior—changing numbers, flipping figures, and throwing loops into problems. In other words, just repeating the math problems you've done before doesn't always result in a good grade on a test—especially if you have a tricky teacher.

When you are studying for a math test, instead of simply doing problems again, be sure to outline each concept that you've learned. That means that you have to **make your own study guide that contains each rule, formula, or theorem that you've learned with a diagram and sample problem**. For example, if you are studying geometry, don't just do a few problems that ask you to figure out how many degrees are contained in a shape. Instead, outline each rule (such the number of degrees in a regular polygon is equal to the number of sides minus two times 180° or (n-2) x 180°) so that you understand each kind of shape you will encounter. Even if your teacher asks you how many degrees there are in a 100-sided figure, you'll know how to get the answer. If you just memorize the number of degrees in a triangle, you won't know the answer for other types of shapes. Instead, you need to know the general rule. That way, when the teacher gives you a new kind of shape or flips a shape around, you won't get fazed. You'll know the general rule and be able to apply it to every type of problem.

Real-life strategy: Robbie used to study for math tests by flipping through his textbook and re-doing some problems. While he felt well-prepared, he rarely did well on tests. His teacher would always ask him something he hadn't thought of—for example, he glanced at the different kinds of parallelograms on the review sheet his teacher had distributed. However, he forgot to review how the shapes related to each other, and he hadn't realized that all squares were

rectangles but that not all rectangles were squares. For the next test, he wrote out a study guide that noted each figure and that stated how it related to other shapes. Because he was better able to understand these relationships among the figures by writing them out, this study guide helped him, and he earned a much better grade.

Avoiding Careless Mistakes

You may understand math perfectly but find that you've made careless errors that bring down your grade. Nothing is so depressing as realizing that you understand calculus but added two numbers incorrectly, giving you the wrong answer. Rushing makes you more likely to make mistakes. You might feel so worried about finishing your tests that you rush though the problems and don't pay attention to signs or to your calculations. Here are some ways to reduce your chances of making mistakes on math tests:

Tip #1: Underline or highlight signs.

Using a bright highlighter to make sure you take note of signs helps you slow down. On each problem, use your highlighter pen to highlight (or your pencil to underline) signs such as +, -, *, and /. Highlighting helps you pay attention to negative signs as well. This simple technique can also be used for word problems. Use your highlighter to call attention to important parts of problems. Note the example below:

Televisions at Ray's Electronics go on sale for <u>40%</u> off. If they now cost $50, what was the <u>original price</u>? If the sales price is further discounted by **<u>20%, what would their price be</u>**?

Underlining or highlighting key parts of this question helps you to understand that there are two parts of the answer. First, you have to find the ORIGINAL PRICE—not the sales price—of televisions that have been discounted by 40%. Then, you have to take 20% off the sales price and find that figure. You have to carefully figure out two answers, and it's hard to keep track of what you need to find without underlining.

Tip #2: Use graph paper and paper with plenty of answer space.

Graph paper helps you line up your columns so you make fewer mistakes adding and subtracting. This technique is especially important if you have bad handwriting. In addition, don't cram your work into little spaces on your paper. Although many students think it's virtuous to save paper and be environmentally friendly, such strategies may not help your math grade. If you need to use the backs of papers so that you have enough space to work out your math problems, do so. In addition, be sure to circle your answer so you can find it later.

Tip #3: Speak the steps to yourself.

Many students find that speaking to themselves during tests helps reduce errors. That doesn't mean that you have to appear to be crazy. There is a subtle way in which you can make sure you are reminding yourself to pay attention to your problems by speaking softly to yourself during tests. For example, you can softly speak aloud all the steps in a long division problem to yourself. This strategy might help you retain your focus and not skip a step.

Tip#4: Put your important formulas or other information at the top of the page.

Many students do this step as soon as they receive a math test from their teacher. They know, for example, that they might forget that the angles in a triangle=180 degrees or that any number to the zero power is 1. They need to write these basic rules (angles in a triangle=180°) on top of the page so they don't forget them.

Check-in: Can you use any of these strategies to avoid making careless mistakes on math tests?

_____

_____

_____

_____

Dealing with "Math Anxiety" and Avoiding Rushing

Math tests can be among the most anxiety-producing events in a student's life. As I said above, taking a math test can be like traveling to a foreign country where you simply don't speak the language. You think you understand the material, but then you glance at a page filled with strange symbols that fill you with dread. As a result, you may try to rush through the test, making mistakes because you aren't pacing yourself appropriately. Here are some ways to diffuse the tension and show your teacher what you truly know.

Tip #1: Go to what you know.

If you feel anxious when you sit down to take a math test, skim over the page to find a problem you understand. If you start with material you feel confident about, you will feel calmer attacking the problems that you feel less certain about. Kind teachers may start off the test with a warm-up question that's a little easier to make you feel more relaxed, but this isn't always true. There's no rule against working on a later problem and coming back to earlier questions later, when you feel more confident.

Tip #2: Start working—and show your work.

Some students have a hard time starting to work, but once they do, they find that they understand more about a math problem than they initially thought. You may be the kind of student who has a hard time diving in, but, once you're in, you can't stop yourself. Push yourself to start working on a problem, and you may find yourself immersed in the material and forgetting all about your jitters.

Remember that many math teachers give partial credit for showing your work. That means they are often more interested in how you think about the problem than the result. Be sure to show as much work as you can, as clearly as you can. Even if you don't get the answer right, you may get a lot of credit for your work and do better than you think.

Tip #3: Skim over the test and get an overview.

Before you start working, you may want to look over the entire test to acquaint yourself with the number and kinds of problems. This will help you pace yourself on the test and spend the right amount of time on each type of problem. Estimate how much time you'll need for later problems and pace yourself so that you make sure you can get to the last problem. If running out of time seems to be a constant problem for you, you may need to apply to your school for extra time on tests. See the chapter on "Getting and Using Accommodations" for more information about how to apply for extra time.

Tip #4: Ask your teacher about confusing wording.

Though they may not always admit it, teachers are mere mortals. They sometimes word questions in a confusing or awkward way, and it's usually perfectly acceptable to ask your teacher during a test to clarify the directions for a certain type of problem. Mind you, this doesn't mean that you can ask your teacher for the answer. However, you may be able to ask if you are approaching the problem correctly.

Tip #5: When all else fails, remember to breathe.

If you feel like you are getting into a very panicked state and not thinking straight, a deep breath or two may enable you to relax. Take less than a minute to collect your thoughts and remember that you've taken many math tests before—and will do so again—so one test isn't going to kill you. If you put this test into its proper context, you may find it easier to relax. Remember that a test is nothing more than a sheet of paper with problems you've already studied on it. It's not a measure of your worth or value. Just approach the test the way you would a video game—go through each problem with a clear mind, confident you can figure out a way to defeat the enemy and rack up points.

Check-in: Can you apply any of these relaxation techniques to your math tests?

_____

_____

_____

Chapter 6:
Useful for *Jeopardy*:
Mastering Tests that Require Memorization

Preparing for History Tests

If you are like many students, you can remember all the words to your favorite songs, every line of your favorite movies, and every statistic about your favorite sports team. However, when it comes to memorizing names and dates for history tests, your brain completely fails you. Part of the problem may be that the information means nothing to you. If the Nullification Crisis of the 1830s doesn't mean anything to you, it may be difficult to recall all the details. Here are some strategies to help you master the immense amount of details involved in most middle and high school history tests. As you read over the strategies, be sure to consider how you can adapt them to your specific learning style (auditory, kinesthetic, or visual) that you learned about in the first chapter.

Tip #1: Using an active approach, fit the details into a larger story.

Remember that history is a story. If you can tell the larger story, you are more likely to remember the details. For example, the Nullification Crisis of 1832-1833 in South Carolina—when South Carolina refused to pay a kind of import tax called a tariff—means very little unless you connect it to the larger problems southern states at the time were having with the federal government in Washington, D.C. Instead of studying each little detail, fit them into a larger story or theme—such as on-going problems the south was having being part of the United States. Then, you can list events that led up to the Civil War and fit them into a larger story. Remembering events in a larger story is far easier than trying to remember each detail or event in isolation.

This approach requires you to be a more active studier. Instead of simply looking over the textbook or your notes, you need to make your own study guide. In your study guide, write out the main ideas yourself and list the details under each main idea.

SAMPLE HISTORY STUDY GUIDE

Reasons the North won the Civil War (summary of pages 156-163, 180-190 in textbook)

North:

– superior manpower: 22 million in population (vs. 9 million in South)

– more money: Lincoln used income tax to raise money (see p. 181)

– more industry: 10 times industry of South (see p. 159)

South:

– south had problems with authority, causing them to lose war

    – Nullification: right of each state to disagree with fed. government

        – earlier Nullification Crisis (page 145)

    – West Virginia broke away in 1863

    – Southerners didn't like Jefferson Davis

    – Southerners wanted to keep slaves, not send them to fight

This study guide could boil down a lot of the information in your textbook about the Civil War. Notice that instead of studying each little detail about the North and South separately, the person who wrote out this study guide is fitting the information together like pieces in a larger puzzle. Now, the student will remember why the North won the Civil War, even if that information is scattered throughout her notes or textbook.

Tip #2: Review your history notes and textbook on a regular basis.

This is the main point of this entire book. If you break down your studying into smaller bits, you will remember more information and do better on tests. Most students simply can't remember everything by cramming the night before a test. Studying your notes and textbook regularly is an important part of preparing for history tests. There is simply too much information to cram it all into your head at once. If you study for ten minutes on the bus or each night after class, you will remember the information better over time. Be sure to review your notes shortly after you take them, when they are fresh in your mind. If there is any information in the notes that isn't clear, you want to clarify your notes so that you can understand them when you refer to them later. If you wait too long to review your notes, you won't always remember what your notes mean or what the teacher was talking about in class.

If you are visual learner, incorporate color into your notes to make them easier to understand. Highlight information such as people, dates, and other historical terms in one color, and use another color for themes—or larger ideas that bring together the information.

Some teachers lecture on the textbook and add additional information in class. One way you can take notes on the textbook and make them consistent with class notes is to use a spiral-bound notebook. On the left-hand page, take notes from your textbook. On the right-hand page, take notes from class that relate to the reading. See the example below for more information. This format allows you to study both your textbook and notes at the same time.

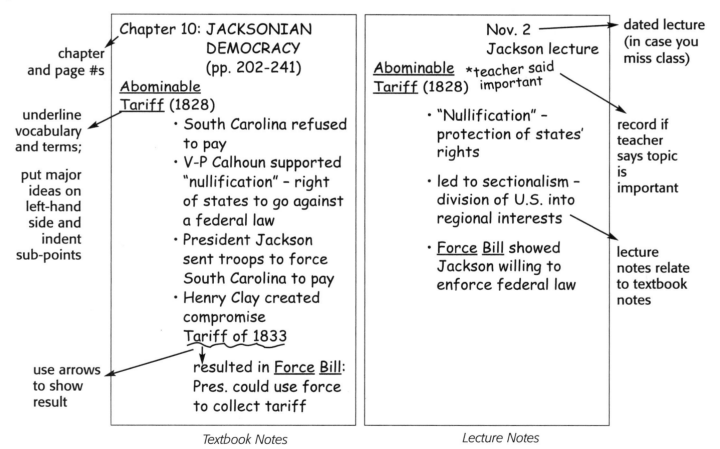

Textbook Notes   Lecture Notes

Tip #3: Ask your teacher the format of the test beforehand.

The process of studying for a matching test is different than that of studying for an essay test. Be sure to ask your teacher the format of your history test in advance. Knowing information well enough to recognize it on a matching test is very different than studying it well enough to be able to answer short answer, fill-in-the-blank, or essay questions. If you need to know the information in a more in-depth way, be sure to not only recognize it but be able to recall it from memory.

Tip #4: Use your favorite study strategy in history.

Although your teacher may use a primarily visual approach—for example, putting information on the board, you can study in a way that uses your preferred technique. For example, if you are an auditory learner, put the information into a song. If you are visual learner, use acronyms to remember information (for example, make a word or saying out the first letter of the names of each of the eight U.S. Presidents) and write out the acronym. If you are a kinesthetic learner, pretend to be a figure in history and act out your role, or sort through flash cards with the information you need to know written on them.

Real-life strategy: Though she spent a lot of time studying, 9th grader Margaret found that she couldn't lift her grades above the "B" level in history. She used the study guides with each historical term and person that her teacher gave her, and she looked over these guides many times before tests. However, she made mistakes on the multiple-choice questions on the test, and she found that she left a lot of information out of essay tests. In addition, her history teacher said that her thesis statements on tests were too simplistic. Margaret's World History teacher recommended that instead of simply looking over study guides that Margaret instead make her own study guides with the themes—or larger issues—in each chapter. Instead of simply looking over the names of Enlightenment philosophers, Margaret made her own study guide that included the main idea of the Enlightenment. On this study guide, she listed each of the philosophers and his major ideas. Although her teacher hadn't told the students the short-answer and essay questions before the test, Margaret received an "A" on her Enlightenment test because she was prepared to explain the ideas of the period on the essay question and to answer detailed short-answer, matching, and true-and-false questions about each figure in history.

CHECK-IN: What are some useful strategies you could use to study for history tests?

_____

_____

_____

_____

How to Study for Science Tests

Science tests require memorization of both terms and sometimes formulas. Each type of problem requires a slightly different strategy, but again, the strategies require you to look over your notes and textbook on a regular, if not daily, level.

Tip #1: Keep a list of all the new vocabulary you need to know.

Some textbooks list vocabulary that you need to know in bold letters and at the end of each chapter. However, as you move on in school, you may encounter a textbook that doesn't list all the new vocabulary. In either case, be sure to study all your new terms on a regular basis. You should take a complete set of notes in class and write down everything your teacher notes on the board or presents in a PowerPoint. If you can't always catch everything your teacher is saying, be sure to get a set of complete notes from another student. Highlight the vocabulary terms presented in class and in your textbook, and study them on a nightly or nearly nightly level by using flash cards or simply writing them on a piece of paper.

Tip #2: Be sure to study diagrams.

A lot of scientific information can be nicely summarized in pictures and diagrams. For example, if you are studying the respiratory system, you can learn the information by studying a diagram instead of simply reading over each step in your textbook. Be sure to practice labeling and understanding diagrams in your textbook or in notes or handouts your teacher gives you in class. This strategy is particularly fitting for students who are visual learners. Diagrams often show up on science tests, and if you know not only the words in your notes and textbook but also the diagrams and charts, you will fare better on tests.

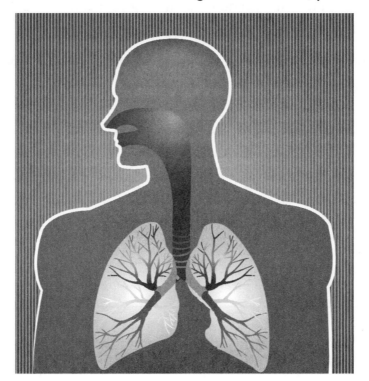

Tip #3: Understand labs and use them while studying.

Science teachers don't make you do lab work just so that they can see frogs dissected. Instead, they want you to connect this work to what you are learning in the class, whether it's understanding how a toy car accelerates down a ramp or how different chemicals react when combined. As you carry out lab work, be sure to think about how it reinforces the material in your textbook and classroom discussions. In addition, when you are studying for tests, be sure to review the lessons of your lab work. Often, teachers will require you to know the material in the analysis section of labs, and they may also require that you know the diagrams and other work you produce during labs.

This strategy is particularly important if you are the type of student who needs to understand material by doing actual physical work. In other words, labs are especially well suited for the kinesthetic learner who learns by doing. If you are this type of learner, don't ignore this opportunity to use your hands to understand the material more fully.

Tip #4: Practice problems using formulas.

Some science tests also ask you to remember and use formulas, for example $D = RT$ (or distance = rate x time). These types of problems can be part of your test, in addition to knowing the meaning of vocabulary words. Therefore, be sure to include all of the formulas you need to know on your study guide. Write out each formula and then do practice problems that use this formula. It's important to know both the formula and to practice it using the problems you covered for homework or for class. Often, teachers will give you a variation or twist on your homework problems on the test.

If you have **poor handwriting**, you may want to use graph paper for science problems, as you can in math class. Using graph paper, especially paper with larger boxes, will allow you to align your columns and remind you to leave space between each number, making your work easier to read and helping you avoid making careless mistakes.

CHECK-IN: What are some new strategies that you think you can use to study for science tests?

_____

_____

_____

_____

_____

Studying for Foreign Language Tests

Preparing for tests in foreign languages requires a lot of different skills depending on the type of test. Some tests are quite simple and only require you to know vocabulary; however, as you advance in school, you are often required to master more complicated grammar and reading in another language. Here are some tips you may find helpful as you study ***español, français***, or another foreign language. There are also tips for learning **Mandarin (a Chinese dialect)**, as more and more students in the United States are studying this important language. Because Mandarin uses special characters, it presents different obstacles and requires slightly different study techniques.

Vocabulary tests

For Romance languages: Customize your favorite study technique.

If you are a **visual learner**, you can use strategies such as note cards with different colors for masculine and feminine words. In other words, put feminine words on a pink note card (or any other color that makes sense to you—you need not be traditional) and all masculine words on a blue note card (or any other different color).

There are creative ways to incorporate learning the pronunciation of the word into your studying. For example, you can record the pronunciation of the word onto an MP3 player and listen to it as you study. This technique is very good for **auditory learners**. You want to make sure that you look at the word you are learning while listening to its pronunciation.

A key to learning a language is practice. Therefore, be sure to review vocabulary regularly until you get it, and go back and review earlier words that you may have forgotten. While you may not be able to travel to a country that speaks the language you are studying, cable TV offers great opportunities for watching shows in that language. You can watch a show and write down the words you don't know to look them up later. There are also radio programs broadcast in foreign languages, so check with your teacher about the opportunities in your neighborhood to practice the language outside of class. The more you listen to the language, the better you will do.

For Mandarin:

Mandarin requires that you study characters along with *pinyin* (phonetic English spelling of Chinese words) and English translations. The best way to learn all three elements at once is to make flash cards that include the Chinese character and *pinyin* on one side and the English translation on the other. There are also computer software programs that allow you to practice writing characters, so ask your Chinese teacher which he or she recommends.

The problem for many beginning Mandarin students is that they can't use the Chinese dictionary until they learn more character roots, as using the dictionary involves knowing roots of characters rather than simply looking up words alphabetically. Ask your teacher about how to work around this problem. Many students start compiling their own word lists in the manner mentioned above—with flash cards that contain the character and *pinyin* on one side and the English translation on the other. You want to review your characters regularly, making sure that you master roots that will help you with other characters.

Grammar: Practice Makes Perfect

Foreign language learners need to approach grammar systematically. That is, each time you learn a new grammar concept, be sure to master it before moving on. There are several websites that offer additional practice in grammar in Spanish and French. Two general sites are the following:

For Spanish: http://www.spanish4all.com

For French: http://www.uni.edu/becker/newfrench.html

These websites will provide you with additional practice for elements of grammar you need to master. On some of the sites, you can practice verb conjugations.

The way to do well on grammar tests in a foreign language is to practice regularly—even in advance of the test. If you are learning a tricky verb conjugation, write out all the forms of the verb until you get it right. You can also use the websites mentioned above to review grammar regularly. You should be sure to note exactly which grammar concepts you are getting incorrect on tests, quizzes, and in-class exercises. Then practice these concepts regularly until you master them.

Reading: Bringing all Your Skills Together

If you are in an advanced foreign-language class, you will have to read in that language. Tests that ask you to read in a foreign language or to answer questions about your reading are particularly difficult because they require you to have mastered vocabulary and grammar. As you read, you need to make sure you look up all the words you don't know and keep a running list on a sheet of paper or computer file. Although this work will take you a lot of time at first, it will eventually get easier as you build your vocabulary.

If you have trouble reading in the language, be sure to review each passage with your teacher. Try to analyze exactly why you don't understand the material. If it's because of your vocabulary, follow the advice above and look up each word you don't know. Read with a dictionary, and you will find it easier going after a while. If grammar's getting in your way, isolate exactly which grammatical concepts you don't understand and use practice exercises in class, your textbook, and on the grammar websites listed above until you master them. If you struggle to read in English, you may want to see if there is a tape of the book you are reading in a foreign language to assist you.

CHECK-IN:

Which techniques will you use to learn vocabulary in a foreign language?

_____

_____

_____

_____

Which techniques will you use to learn grammar in that language?

_____

_____

_____

_____

If you are struggling with reading in a foreign language, what is getting in your way?

_____

_____

_____

_____

Which strategies will you use to overcome the obstacle to your reading?

_____

_____

_____

_____

Chapter 7:
Taking the Sting Out of Pop Quizzes

How to Be Prepared through Regular Review

Although some "pop" quizzes are truly surprises, most of the time, your teacher gives you an idea beforehand that he or she might give a quiz in the next few days to make sure the class is up-to-date with the reading and the homework. You want to make sure that you listen in class to these types of cues and don't get caught off guard by a quiz you weren't expecting.

In addition, you obviously want to keep up with the material of the class, including regular review of your class notes and reading. Each night, time permitting, you should spend ten minutes reviewing your class notes and underlining key concepts. Information is best consolidated in your mind if you review regularly, particularly shortly after the class has taken place. ***Again, you will be most successful if you review on a regular basis***, and you will find that you are better prepared for larger tests if you keep up with your work each week. There are of course those times when you find that you have so much work that you can't dedicate time to reviewing class notes. However, you may also find little pockets of time, such as when you are watching TV or sitting on the bus, that allow you to review for a few minutes and keep up with the class material without ruining your life.

Maintaining Your Cool

It's easy to get flustered when your teacher pops a quiz on you. Although you may feel rushed for time, be sure to take a second to try to regain your balance. Try some of the deep breathing techniques you might use to deal with anxiety on other kinds of tests. Look over the questions and try to write something down—even if you aren't sure of the answer. Usually, teachers grade these kinds of tests a bit more leniently than they grade larger, announced tests. Remember that a quiz isn't worth much and even a poor grade won't affect your overall grade that much.

Improving Your Results on Pop Quizzes

If you find that are consistently scoring poorly on pop quizzes, you want to ask yourself why. Look at the reasons below and skim over the potential solutions that you think might help you perform better on surprise quizzes.

_____ You rush through pop quizzes.

Solutions:
- Take a minute to relax at the beginning of the pop quiz.
- Ask your teacher for a few more minutes.
- Skim over the quiz and budget your time more efficiently.

_____ You do your textbook reading and your homework, but you still get questions wrong.

Solutions:

- You need to read more carefully with a highlighter in hand. As you read, summarize the material in the margin.
- Review your reading and notes on a regular basis. Keep lists of all the vocabulary you need to know.

____ You get really nervous when you are presented with a pop quiz.

- Take a minute to breathe before beginning the quiz.
- Remember that your quiz grade isn't worth that much in your larger grade.
- Start with an easier question and work your way to the more difficult questions.
- Clarify any directions you don't understand with the teacher.

Real-life Strategy: Although Ben, a seventh grader, always did the reading for his English class, he had a 60% average on the reading quizzes his teacher gave by surprise every few weeks. Ben enjoyed his reading, but he often saved it for last and read in bed with his headphones on. The next morning, he could recall very little of what he had read the night before. Ben's teacher showed him how to read with a highlighter in hand. Whenever Ben came to a new character or an important scene in the novel or play he was reading, he would highlight it. In addition, after reading each chapter, he would summarize the main events in that chapter in a sentence in the inside cover of his book. He read over his summaries and his highlighter marks in the morning on the way to school. After perfecting these techniques, Ben's reading quiz average went up to an 85%.

Chapter 8:

Winning the Guessing Game:
How to Take Multiple-Choice Tests

Eliminate the Negative

Take the following pop quiz:

When I go to school:

   (a) I am never tired or bored.

   (b) I am often tired or bored.

   (c) I am usually tired or bored.

   (d) I am always tired or bored.

If you answered a, b, c, or d, you could be right. However, the most reasonable answers are (b) and (c). It's unlikely that you are never tired or bored—after all, school can be very tiring and extremely boring. It's similarly unlikely that you are always tired and bored. Don't forget the times you are hanging out with your friends—making plans for the weekend or secretly playing video games on your cell phone. Therefore, you can most likely eliminate the most extreme choices in any list of multiple-choice questions.

Tip #1: Eliminate extreme answer choices.

To answer multiple-choice questions, be sure to eliminate any answers that seem too extreme. Underline words in the answer choices such as "always," "never," or "all" and "none." While these answer choices could be right, they often aren't. Remember the example above? Most answers are in the middle range, so you can get rid of the other choices.

Tip #2: Clearly eliminate wrong answer choices by crossing them out.

Some students like to literally take their pencils and cross out the incorrect answer choices so that can concentrate on the remaining answers. This simple practice allows you to be sure you won't choose an answer that you've already rejected, and it enables you to focus your energy on the choices that remain.

Reading Between the Lines

Take the following pop quiz:

Each of the following is an example of wasted time EXCEPT:

(a) playing video games for four hours

(b) studying for math

(c) watching _Gossip Girl_

(d) Listening to the entire playlist on your iPod

Tip #3: Consider which answer choice is different.

While you may think studying for math tests is actually the best use of time, notice something about the answer choices above. Each of the choices except "B" involves a leisurely activity, while only "B" represents an academic activity. Also, be sure to read the directions for this question. Notice it uses the word "EXCEPT." Therefore, this question involves recognizing which of the answer choices is different. In a way, it doesn't matter what you even know before looking at the answer choices. All you have to do is find the one answer choice that is different than the others.

Now, consider the following more difficult question:

Herbert Hoover was criticized for all of the following EXCEPT:

    (a) Unemployment rose from 1930-1931

    (b) Business leaders did little to solve the nation's economic crisis

    (c) The stock market continued to fall during his presidency

    (d) More people received jobs on construction projects

The truth is that you don't need to know much about Herbert Hoover to get this question right. Even if you don't even know who Herbert Hoover was (he was President during the beginning of the Great Depression in the U.S.), think about the question. It asks you for all the reasons people were angry with Hoover. There is only one reason that could've made people happy. Notice that choices A, B, and C involve things that couldn't possibly make people happy—no one likes rising unemployment, a continued economic crisis, or a falling stock market. Only "D" involves something positive—more people getting jobs. That's most likely the only thing Hoover would have been praised for. Again, this question involves choosing the answer that isn't like the others.

Tip #4: Read the questions and choices carefully.

While this strategy seems obvious, many students get anxious during multiple-choice tests and simply don't read carefully. Use your pencil to underline key words in the question such as "EXCEPT" or "NOT" to make sure you are paying attention to what the question is asking. In addition, notice that often, the correct answer choice for a multiple-choice question appears elsewhere on the test. For example, it could be in a short-answer question. Be sure to read over the test and note when the teacher actually gives you the right answer on the test. Also, take care to record your answer choices correctly, as many students do not carefully write down the answer for each question in the correct order.

Real-life Strategy: Sixth grader Lily knew the material for her history class, but she often answered the multiple-choice questions on tests incorrectly. She didn't read very carefully, and she forgot to pay attention to words such as "EXCEPT." By using her pencil to underline key parts of questions and answer choices, she was able to understand how each choice was different, and she found that she could answer more questions correctly.

CHECK-IN: What are some potential strategies you could use for multiple-choice questions?

_____

_____

_____

Chapter 9:
Standardized Tests:
State-Mandated Tests and College-Entrance Tests

Establishing a Study Schedule

As part of the federal No Child Left Behind law, all students in public schools in grades 3-8 must pass yearly exams in reading, math, and other subjects (some public high school students are also tested). In addition, students applying to colleges must take entrance exams such as the SAT or ACT (although check with your college guidance counselor about the many colleges in the U.S. that do not require these tests). These types of tests are called standardized tests, and although the content differs, they involve mainly answering multiple-choice questions by filling in bubbles. They have become a larger part of life for students in American middle and high schools, though some experts still doubt the tests' ability to judge how much students know.

There are some general techniques you can use to take these tests. First, you should give yourself sufficient time to study for state-mandated tests that you need to pass and for college-entrance exams, including the SAT and ACT. Start by taking a practice test, which will allow you to familiarize yourself with the format and timing of the test and the types of questions that will appear on the test. Then, use your results to analyze which types of questions you are getting wrong—and why.

Address the kinds of questions you're having problems with. There are multiple ways to approach a problem, and you have to find the strategy that works for you. There are many ways around a problem, and just because you are getting a question wrong in practice tests doesn't mean you can't get it right—it may simply mean you haven't found and practiced an approach that works for you.

When you are working on troubleshooting your problem areas, be sure to pay attention to your energy level. Try to study when you are fresh and rested, and **give yourself frequent breaks**. You can't study too much of this stuff without getting burned out, so try to work steadily for an hour, listen to music or otherwise relax for 10 minutes, and then return to studying. If you can break up your studying into shorter study sessions, the strategies will be easier to master.

Pacing on the Test

Pacing on standardized tests is very important. Whether you are taking the test under regular time, or extended time (which is 50% or, in some cases, 100% extra time), be sure to take entire practice tests under timed conditions MANY times before taking the actual test. **It's very important that you take entire practice tests at one sitting—particularly if you have extended time**. Many students have taken practice tests only a few sections at a time and then found that the actual test wore them out. In addition, if your mind has a hard time making transitions between sections, you need to practice doing so. The actual test will ask you to make many transitions—between sections and between different kinds of questions in the same section. The most important tactic to remember is **not to get hung up on any one question**, which is not that important in the context of your overall score.

A Note on Guessing: Find out how each test you take is scored. For example, on the SAT, you are penalized ¼ point for each question you answer incorrectly. Therefore, you should guess if you can eliminate one or two of the answer choices. For math grid-ins, there is no penalty for guessing, though the probability that you'd guess the right number correctly and fill it in is quite low. So, work quickly in areas where you feel confident and move on from areas you don't know.

Real-life Strategy: David had 50% extended time and studied for the SAT by taking practice tests only one section at a time. When he took the actual SAT, he found that he scored well below his practice tests because he wasn't used to sitting down and concentrating for nearly 6 hours. He also was thrown by having to make constant transitions between sections. He was helped before his second SAT by practicing the entire test under timed conditions and making sure that he could focus and sit for that period of time.

How to Calm Down and Not Rush

Though you may be anxious taking standardized tests, **try not to rush**. If you are the kind of student who rushes through your work, try the following strategies to prevent speeding on the test:

- put your pencil down after each problem in the math section or each passage in the reading section
- make sure you underline important parts of reading passages to make your mind slow down and concentrate on the material
- underline important parts of math questions such as "EXCEPT" or the solution the question asks for to ensure that you are answering the question correctly
- take a deep breath and put your pencil down when you get to a new reading section or math section
- stretch during breaks and eat energy-sustaining snacks such as yogurt and fruit and power bars instead of candy bars and cookies

A Note on Bubbling in Answers

Some students have experienced the worst nightmare on standardized tests—they realized that they knew a lot of the right answers but their bubbling in was incorrect. That is, they filled in the wrong bubbles or got off track by one question when filling in answers. DON'T LET THS HAPPEN TO YOU. Be sure to "subvocalize"—that is, speak under you breath—each time you bubble in an answer. Say to yourself, "this is question one, and I'm bubbling in the answer for question 1." It may seem simplistic, but this technique helps you stay on track and get the score you deserve.

A Note on Medication

If you take any kinds of medication for ADD or other conditions, make sure you take the right dose on the day of the test. Please see your doctor with any questions about your medication. Many students who do not have ADD believe that taking a dose of stimulant medications such as Ritalin on the morning of the test will help them. **It has not been proven that taking stimulants helps people who haven't been diagnosed by a professional and who haven't been prescribed medication by a medical doctor.** In addition to the medical risks (and illegal nature) of taking medication that you haven't been prescribed, you shouldn't try anything new on the day of the test. Preparing for the test sufficiently over time is the only medication you need.

Gaining Confidence and Overcoming Procrastination

If you find it difficult to get started studying for the standardized test you have to take, it's completely understandable. Taking standardized tests isn't generally one of life's greater pleasures, and even top scorers are intimidated before the test. It's natural to have jitters or just be tired of the whole thing, and it's understandable that you don't want to study—particularly if you are in the midst of a busy year in school. You may find yourself restless, anxious, and bored while studying and therefore put it off.

The most important strategy to overcome procrastination is to gain confidence in your ability to understand and outwit the test. As you take more and more practice tests and find strategies in this book that work for you, you will find it easier to be confident. If you find it difficult to start studying, you may want to work with a friend. Arrange to meet weekly and force yourselves to study for at least an hour at a time. Reward yourself for studying with immediate results—such as an hour listening to music, playing a video game, or shooting hoops.

Break up your studying into short, frequent sessions. After each study session, try to find time to do something that revives you. Don't try to cram everything into your head at once—you will stress yourself out, and you won't be able to retain the information as well as if you study for short periods of time.

Try to find a creative way to approach problems. For example, one student made a game out of shuffling and reshuffling her vocabulary cards. Although she still would have rather watched TV than study, she found that she was motivated to study vocabulary by making a game out of throwing down cards and seeing if she knew the definitions of the words. By using this strategy, she improved her vocabulary in only a few months. Use your own intelligence and creativity to come up with strategies and games that will motivate you to study.

Real-life Strategy: Gabriel found he had energy to study for his 8th grade state-wide math test because he saw it as a game. Each time he learned a new strategy or mastered a new kind of question, he saw himself becoming better and better at the game. Rather than regarding the test as an obstacle, he saw merely as a kind of puzzle that he could unlock (and, as it turns out, score very well on).

Real-life Strategy: Michael gained confidence in his ability to do well on his SAT by analyzing his PSAT scores. While his overall scores were good—not great—and not close to what he wanted, he realized that he had gotten almost every question he answered right. He applied for and received extended time from the College Board, and, after taking many practice tests, he went into the SAT with confidence. Michael knew that with extended time, he would do well. He had the skills to get a high score, and it was only a matter of having more time to show what he knew. He was right—his scores on the SAT were significantly higher than those on the PSAT.

Chapter 10:
Getting and Using Accommodations in School

Which Accommodations are Right for You?

Accommodations refer to changes in the way you learn in class or modifications in the way you take tests that help you show what you know. Many people think that accommodations are a form of "cheating," but in reality, they simply mean getting the assistance you need to reach your true potential. They don't involve "dumbing down" your work or making your work easier. Instead, getting and using accommodations is like finding out that you have less than 20/20 vision and need glasses to see perfectly.

There is no weakness in asking your school for the modifications you need, as long as you promise to live up to your end of the bargain and work hard to achieve everything you are capable of doing.

The process for getting accommodations varies depending on your school. Some schools are willing to make more changes simply because you request them, while others will require you to go through an evaluation by a psychologist or other qualified professional at your school or outside your school to be sure that you need these kinds of assistance.

Many students know that some people at their schools receive extended time on tests. This accommodation isn't the same thing as getting "untimed tests." Instead, it allows students to get extra time on tests. However, there are many other kinds of accommodations that can help you, and it's important to select the accommodation that will really work with your challenges. Here is a list of some common challenges and the way successful students have slightly modified their regular school programs to meet these challenges. Remember that this list isn't complete and that any accommodations you receive require the approval of your school.

Problem: You run out of time on timed tests and quizzes.

Possible solutions and accommodations: You want to make sure you are using your time wisely. Be sure to use the strategies for pacing mentioned in other chapters, including glancing over the entire test before beginning and planning ahead in your mind how you will complete the test on time. If these strategies don't work, you may want to request testing from your school that verifies that you need extra time on tests.

Problem: You have illegible handwriting that interferes with math and other tests.

Possible solutions and accommodations: Poor handwriting often means that you can't keep your columns aligned for math and science tests. Some solutions to this problem include using graph paper that forces you to put one number into each box. In addition, you can use larger paper that gives you more space to write. In essay tests, you should skip lines when writing to make your work more legible. Finally, you may want to ask your school for the accommodation of using a computer for quizzes and tests that require a lot of writing, if there are computers available at your school.

Problem: You can't absorb a lot of the information presented in class lectures.

Possible solutions and accommodations: You should ask a classmate for notes from class. If you can't find suitable class notes from a fellow student, explain to the teacher that you are trying to absorb the information but can't always do so. Ask the teacher, the learning specialist, or the psychologist at your school if they can help you attain a set of notes. With the permission of the teacher, you can also record class lectures and listen to them later. You may need testing to document that you can't always pick up information in class.

Problem: You find that try as you might, you can't sit still and concentrate during long stretches of time.

Possible solutions and accommodations: You need to take advantage of the time between classes to stretch and get some exercise. In addition, you may need to take breaks during long tests to walk around. You may find that you concentrate better if you sit in the front of the classroom, where there are fewer distractions from fellow students and you are closer to the teacher. You may also be able to take your tests in smaller rooms alone or with a smaller group to minimize distractions. If you have particular concerns, be sure to consult the psychologist or other staff at your school.

Problem: You understand the material, but you often read questions incorrectly on tests.

Possible solutions and accommodations: Some teachers may be willing to read the directions aloud to you. Others may substitute a written portion of the exam with an oral portion that allows you to show what you know. Be sure to read the directions carefully—underline key words such as "EXCEPT" and "NOT."

Real-life Strategy: Eighth grader Julia studied very diligently for tests and knew the material backward and forward when her mother quizzed her about it aloud. However, when she took written tests in history and Spanish, she received really poor grades. She had almost given up hope when she had an oral exam in Spanish on which she received a 100%. She realized that she was an auditory thinker—while she had trouble at times processing written information, she understand information presented orally perfectly. After making this discovery, she asked her teachers to read directions and multiple-choice questions aloud. She slowly moved toward reading questions herself by underlining key parts of questions, such as "EXCEPT" and making sure she understood directions by checking with her teachers during tests. She found that her studying now paid off, and she received much better grades that reflected how hard she had worked.

Problem: You actually understand math, but you make a lot of careless mistakes and often add 1+1 incorrectly.

Possible solutions and accommodations: Believer it or not, a lot of math geniuses make mistakes with simple math calculations. Some students also have a hard time remembering rote facts such as additions and subtraction facts. Possible solutions to these issues including underlining math signs and other important parts of math questions. In addition, some math teachers allow students to use calculators for simpler math calculations.

Check-In: Which accommodation or accommodations do you need?

_____

_____

_____

_____

_____

Be sure to check with your school about how to ask for accommodations.

Using Your Accommodations Wisely

If your school has granted you accommodations, the school has done some of its part in helping you live up to your potential. Now, it's your turn to help yourself show what you are capable of. That doesn't mean that you are now free to relax and think that the accommodation you have—whether it's extended time on tests or use of graph paper on a math test for poor handwriting—will take care of your performance. The school has given you the opportunity to show what you know on tests, but you have to know the material and continue to work hard. Only the combination of good preparation and smart accommodations that are right for you will allow you to work up to your potential.

In addition, having accommodations may mean that you have to ask your teachers for what you need each time you take a test. You may have to remember to tell your teacher that you have extra time and arrange a time to come back to finish the test. You may be responsible for bringing graph paper or whatever else you need to the test. Having accommodations imposes certain responsibilities on you, and you have to live up to them. In addition, you have to ask for what you need. You may at times feel embarrassed about asking for testing conditions that are different from what other students use. However, you wouldn't be embarrassed asking your teacher for permission to put on your eyeglasses. Using accommodations is similar to wearing glasses—some students need them and others don't, but wearing them isn't like cheating. Glasses simply help you show what you know. If you need them, you wear them. If you need accommodations, you should use them.

Another consideration when you use accommodations is that doing so may at times make your testing longer. For example, if you have 50% extended time on tests, you are going to spend more time working. While this accommodation may help you finish your tests, remember that it may also make you feel more tired because your test will last longer. In addition, some students use their extra time to write more on essay tests—usually material that they don't need. Instead, after you finish your regular time, you want to use your extra time to go back to revise and correct your writing.

Real-life strategy: When 9th grader Stephen started using his extra time on English and history tests with long essay questions, he wrote and wrote until his time was up. However, he found *that he often included material that was outside the scope of the question and that didn't really help his grade. Because he had dyslexia, he often made spelling and grammar mistakes that caused his overall essay grades to go down. Instead of using his extra time to write longer essays, he used the time to go back and review his writing. He corrected grammar, spelling, and punctuation before he handed in his test, and he read over the whole essay to make sure he hadn't left any material out and to ensure that the essay was well-organized. Stephen found that these techniques helped improve the quality and grades of his essay exams.*

Applying for Accommodations on College-Entrance Exams:

The SAT and ACT

If you have a learning issue or suspect you do, you can petition the College Board for accommodations—or special testing conditions—for the SAT I, the SAT II, and the AP. You can also contact the ACT if you choose to take this college-entrance test. ***You should consult with staff at your school and your parents at each stage described below***. The College Board and ACT offer some students 50% (and, in some cases, 100%) extended time on standardized tests based on evidence of the students' learning or physical disabilities. The College Board and ACT also offer some test-takers breaks as needed and use of a computer to write essays on the SAT I, ACT, and on other tests.

The first step in pursuing these types of accommodations is to have a thorough educational evaluation by the psychologist at your school or by an outside professional. Again, you should consult with your school about how to pursue this evaluation, as it has to conform to certain guidelines (published under "Services for Students with Disabilities" on the College Board website at www.collegeboard.com or on the ACT website at www.actstudent.org). Be aware that each testing organization has slightly different requirements about testing, including how recent the documentation must be. ***In each case, be sure to double-check all information in this book with information on their websites, as their requirements change each academic year.***

After you are evaluated to document evidence of your learning disability, you must submit the evaluation to the College Board or ACT far in advance of the date on which you want to take a standardized test. Be sure to consult the College Board's and ACT's websites about the deadlines for submitting your documentation. **However, simply submitting the documentation doesn't mean that you will receive the accommodations you ask for. Generally, the College Board and ACT are more likely to grant you accommodations if you have already received these accommodations—such as 50% extended time on tests or use of a computer for writing essays—from your school and have used them for many school months (check the websites for more information).** If your school has granted you these accommodations and you have used them for the period of time regulated by these test organizations, staff at your school who handle students with disabilities can submit your request for accommodations directly to the College Board or ACT in a confidential manner.

If the College Board or ACT grants you accommodations, your use of these accommodations will be totally confidential. The colleges you apply to will not know that you have used them on the SAT or ACT, so you don't have to worry about jeopardizing your chances at college admission.

If you have 50% extended time on the SAT or ACT, be sure to note that extended time does not mean you can spend your time any way you want. You have extended time on each section, but you cannot return to a section if you finish another section before the time is up.

Remember also that having extended time means that the entire test administration will be quite lengthy—**close to six hours (for the SAT and for the ACT with essay)**. You should take practice tests under extended time conditions and pace yourself for a long test day. Many test-takers find that the length of the test eventually interferes with their ability to concentrate, so you should be sure to bring energy-giving snacks and to take advantage of the short breaks you are given.

If the College Board or ACT grants you use of a computer for writing the essay, be sure you know the instructions for using the computer beforehand. Practice writing your essay on a computer rather than writing it by hand. **While you are writing, be sure to save your work often**. You don't want to lose your essay if your computer crashes.

Chapter 11:
Using Your Results to Improve

How to Use Your Results to Get Better

Test results are important tools in making yourself better. Even if you don't get the scores you want, your test and your teachers' comments are tools—even gifts—that you can use to improve your scores the next time. Think of a less-than-ideal test score not merely as a disappointment that you should crumple up and throw into the deepest recesses of your backpack but instead as a guide to help you do better the next time around.

After you've recovered from the test—perhaps a few days later when the sting of your score has gone out of your mind but the material is still somewhat fresh to you—sit down with your test and possibly with your teacher to analyze the exact nature of your errors. What kinds of mistakes did you make, and why do you think you made them? For each kind of mistake, go back to the chapters in this book that deals with that specific type of question or test. Then, come up with some potential strategies to help you.

ANALYSIS OF MISTAKES AND STRATEGIES TO CORRECT THEM

Use this checklist to help guide your analysis:

_____ I made a lot of careless mistakes, for example in math.

Potential strategies: Use a calculator (if allowed in math), underline signs and important words in word problems, align your columns more neatly using graph paper, be sure to go back to check your work.

_____ I read the directions incorrectly.

Potential strategies: The next time you have a similar type of test, underline key parts of the directions. Be sure to clarify the directions with your teacher before you start. In addition, you can sometimes ask your teacher ahead of time what the directions will be for each section of an upcoming test so you are not taken by surprise.

_____ I simply didn't understand the material, though I thought I did.

Potential strategies: Be sure to ask your teacher how to review for the next test. Meet with your teacher and fellow students for review sessions. Go through the material several days in advance of the next test so you can ask questions in class about what you don't understand.

_____ I wrote a sloppy essay exam that included bad grammar and spelling.

Potential strategies: Be sure to review grammar, using the books recommended in the "Helpful Books and Websites" section at the end of the book. Review each kind of grammar mistake you made, and learn the way to correct it. During the next test, incorporate what you learned.

_____ I simply ran out of time.

Potential strategies: Look over the whole test the next time around and budget your time efficiently. Perhaps attack the areas you think will take the most time first, leaving the easier parts for later. Possibly ask your teacher for a few extra minutes for the next test.

Getting Your Parents off Your Back

Parents worry—that's what they do for a living. If you aren't doing as well in school as you want to (and perhaps your parents want you to do), your parents may be constantly pestering you. Even if you take a trip to get a Coke during a long study session, they may attack you like a school of piranhas until you return to your desk and hit the books again.

What's a student to do? One way to possibly get your parents to stop bothering you is to let them know you have a strategy for improving. You want to use your results and sit down with your teacher to produce a strategy you think will help you improve. Then, you can calmly tell your parents that you think you've come up with a way to help you do better. Of course, this process requires some serious thought on your part. You can't lie to your parents just to get them off your back (well, you can, but it won't work very well). If you haven't found a serious way to improve, lying to your parents will only temporarily remove them from your back. As soon as you perform poorly, they'll be back—and in even worse form!

You want to say something to your folks such as, "I know I haven't been doing well in math so far this quarter. But I just met with my teacher, and we agreed to review the material each Wednesday during my study hall." Many parents (not all) will relax when they think you have a plan and are taking on some of the responsibility for carrying out the plan yourself. If you don't live up to your end of the bargain—such as meeting with your teacher or practicing your French verbs—don't expect them to live up to their end of the bargain by leaving you alone!

Once you start doing better, your parents will most likely back off a bit. If they still need to be involved, give them something to do that is minimally invasive—such as quizzing you after you've already finished studying. That way, they will still feel involved, but you won't have them participate in the serious part of your work.

How to Work with Teachers and Tutors

Getting help when you need it is a critical part of improving. Many students think asking for help shows their weaknesses and flaws to the world. However, it is the truly strong person who can admit when he or she gets something—and when he or she doesn't. Have you ever noticed that pesky student— the one who most likely sits in the front row of class and asks question after question? This person is most likely not the person to whom the material comes naturally. However, this student is often the one who does a lot better than you think she or he does because he or she is constantly asking questions and going to see the teacher for extra help.

Realizing that you need a bit of outside support is only the first part of the equation. You can't waste your teachers' time. Remember that you don't want to annoy them (they grade you, after all), and they have to teach a lot of students. To use your teachers' time well, be sure to set up meetings with them well in advance of tests. Teachers hate being besieged with requests for help at the last minute. Remember that they may not be available simply because you are having a problem.

In addition, be sure to approach your teachers with specific questions. Do NOT simply ask, "What will be on the test?" Or even, "How much do I need to pay you to get the test before I take it?" Teachers don't respond well to those types of flippant remarks. Instead, show them that you have lived up to your end of the deal by practicing the material and determining exactly what you don't understand. Say something such as, "Mr. Picklepot, I have spent many hours reviewing trigonometry, and I understand how to find the measures of missing angles. However, can you spend a minute showing me how to find the measures of missing sides?" Notice that this student showed the teacher that he or she has done some work and only has a limited number of questions. Be sure to work on the material before you meet with your teachers. Even if you don't understand much, you will be able to understand exactly what you don't know and be able to use the teacher's time—and your time—best by zeroing in on specific questions (and getting far above a zero on your test!).

Sometimes, you may find that meeting with a teacher simply doesn't help you or that while it helps you, you still don't really understand the material. At this point, you may want to consider turning to someone else for help. You can ask a former teacher in that subject matter—for example, the great math teacher you had last year. You can also ask your parents for help, but sometimes, you fight too much to make this kind of tutoring work out well. If you have the resources, you may want to consider finding a tutor to help you. **Keep in mind that there are federal funds now to hire tutors if your public school doesn't meet some guidelines of the No Child Left Behind Act**. In other words, if your school doesn't meet federal guidelines for a period of time, the government will pay for tutors for you. Please visit the No Child Left Behind website at www.ed.gov/nclb/landing.jhtml for more information.

Having a tutor doesn't excuse you from doing the work. Some students think that hiring a tutor means that they don't have to pay attention in school or see their teachers for clarification. Nothing could be further from the truth. The best use of a tutor is to back up what you learn at school. Only by bringing the tutor the information from class and the clarification you receive from asking your teacher questions can you use the tutor's best potential to help you.

In addition, the best tutors are there only to help you through a rough spot or to teach you better skills. Like the best teachers, they are there to guide you for a specific period of time and teach you material and test-taking and study strategies so that you can do the work on your own. This means that you need to work alongside your tutor to improve. After all, you aren't going to have a tutor to get you through later life—whether it involves college and/or a job. ***You need to learn how to eventually perform well on your own, and using this book is one of the steps in that direction.***

Check-in: What kinds of help do I need from a teacher and/or tutor?

_____

_____

_____

_____

_____

How will I ask this person for help?

_____

_____

_____

_____

_____

Helpful Books and Websites

The books mentioned below are available at www.amazon.com.

For auditory learners and dyslexics:

Recordings for the Blind and Dyslexic (www.rfbd.org): This organization provides hundreds of thousands of titles, including textbooks, to people with visual impairments and learning disabilities that make it difficult to process written text.

For visual learners:

Inspiration (on the web at www.inspiration.com or by phone at 1-800-877-4292) is a software program that allows you to make semantic maps for writing papers and studying for tests. You can make visual connections between different parts of the material, and the program will turn your map into a traditional outline.

For help with grammar and writing:

• *A Writer's Reference* by Diana Hacker. This guide features handy tabs that point you to elements of grammar, research, and writing. Her website at www. dianahacker.com shows you how to correctly cite sources for research papers.

For improving vocabulary:

• *Vocabulary Cartoons: Building an Educated Vocabulary With Visual Mnemonics* by Sam Burchers, Max Burchers, and Bryan Burchers
• *Picture These SAT Words in a Flash* (500 cards) by Philip Geer
• *Shortcut to Word Power: Essential Latin and Greek Roots and Prefixes* by Allan Sack

For information about learning disabilities and learning issues:

• LD Online: At www.ldonline.org. This website features information about common learning disabilities and learning differences.
• Attention Deficit Disorder Association (ADDA): on the web at www.add.org.
• Children and Adults with Attention Deficit/Hyperactivity Disorder (CHADD) on the web at www.chadd.org
• *Help4ADD@HighSchool* by Kathleen Nadeau, Ph.D.: an easy-to-read book that helps you navigate academic and social life in high school if you have ADD/ADHD.
• *ADD and the College Student: A Guide for High School and College Students with Attention Deficit Disorder* by Patricia O. Quinn, M.D.: a book about how to succeed in high school and college if you have ADD/ADHD.
• ADD WareHouse: At www.addwarehouse.com. This site provides resources for students with ADD and learning issues.

For information about standardized tests:

- www.ed.gov/nclb/landing.jhtml: The official No Child Left Behind website.
- www.collegeboard.com: For information about the SAT and AP tests and programs.
- www.actstudent.org: For information about the ACT.

Summary of What I Learned from this Book:

My primary learning style is (from Chapter 1): _____

   • **potential strategies that use my learning style:** _____

_____

List of my strategies:

• **for time-management:** _____

_____

_____

_____

• **for playing the game of school:** _____

_____

_____

_____

• **for essay tests:** _____

_____

_____

_____

• **for math tests:** _____

_____

_____

_____

• **for tests that require memorization:** _____

_____

_____

history

_____

_____

science

_____

_____

foreign language

_____

• **for multiple choice tests:**

_____

_____

_____

• **for standardized tests:**

_____

_____

_____

What accommodations do I need, if any?

_____

_____

_____

What kinds of help do I need from teachers and/or tutors?

_____

_____

_____

Additional thoughts:

_____

_____

_____

_____

_____

_____

_____

_____

Teacher Worksheets & Classroom Exercises

Exercise #1: Filling out weekly and nightly planners.

Students should fill out copies of the blank weekly planner and nightly to-do list below to organize their work for the week. Each major assignment, such as studying for a test, should be broken down into smaller tasks and assigned on a specific day.

WEEKLY SCHEDULE SHEET   WEEK OF_____

TIME	MONDAY	TUESDAY	WEDNESDAY	THURSDAY	FRIDAY	SATURDAY	SUNDAY
4:00 - 5:00 or earlier							
5:00 - 5:30							
5:30 - 6:00							
6:00 - 6:30							
6:30 - 7:00							
7:00 - 7:30							
7:30 - 8:00							
8:00 - 8:30							
8:30 - 9:00							
9:00 - 9:30							
9:30 - 10:00							
10:00 - 10:30 or after							
AVAILABLE TIME / TIME USED FOR STUDY							

This page may be reproduced for personal use.

GET IT DONE TODAY

Date _____

Priority	Assignment	Date Due	Com-pleted
_____	_____		❑
_____	_____		❑
_____	_____		❑
_____	_____		❑
_____	_____		❑
_____	_____		❑
_____	_____		❑
_____	_____		❑
_____	_____		❑
_____	_____		❑
_____	_____		❑
_____	_____		❑
_____	_____		❑

Reprinted with permission. Leslie Davis, Sandi Sirotowitz, and Harvey C. Parker (1996). Study Strategies Made Easy. Florida: Specialty Press, Inc.

Exercise #2: Practice Essay

Question: Should students wear uniforms to school? Come up with a thesis statement that argues for or against students having to wear uniforms to school. Then, produce three reasons for your argument.

Thesis statement: _____.

Reason #1:_____.

Reason #2:_____.

Reason #3:_____.

Use your thesis statement and three reasons outlined above to produce a full essay that follows the essay template given in Chapter 4.

Introductory paragraph, including background and thesis statement:

Topic sentence for first body paragraph:
Reason #1:

Analysis of reason #1:

Topic sentence for second body paragraph:
Reason #2:

Analysis of reason #2:

Topic sentence for third body paragraph:

Reason #3:

Analysis of reason #3:

Conclusion:

Restatement of thesis:

More important point:

Now, check your work for the following:

- Grammar
- Punctuation
- Spelling
- Correct word choice
- Clarity of thesis
- Connection of reasons to thesis
- Thorough analysis of each reason
- Connection of conclusion to thesis

Exercise #3: Note taking from textbooks and class discussions.

Students should use the two-page notebook format given in Chapter 6. On the left-hand side of the notebook, they should take notes on a chapter in their history or science textbook. Then, they should use the right-hand side to take notes in class that relate to their reading.

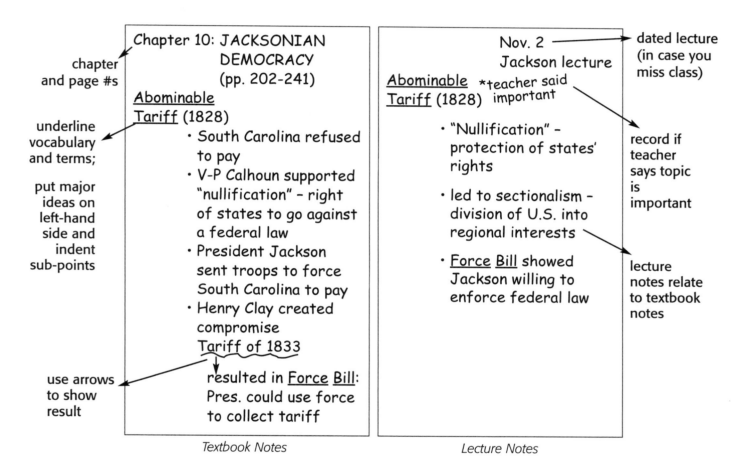

Textbook Notes   Lecture Notes

Grading checklist for notes (mark yes/no and provide comments):

_____ Are the notes complete?

If not, what did student leave out?

_____ Do the notes highlight the important concepts in the chapter?

If not, what should the student have highlighted?

_____ Do the students' class notes correspond to the textbook notes?

_____ Are the notes legible?

_____ Did the student clearly note any questions he or she had about the material?

_____ Did the student properly date the notes and include page numbers in the textbook?

_____ Other?

Exercise #4: Multiple Choice Questions.

You can answer these multiple-choice questions without any background knowledge. Instead, use your ability to read carefully and read between the lines to answer the questions. Be sure to read the questions carefully. The answers and explanations follow.

1. Why was John F. Kennedy a popular U.S. President?
   a. He was involved in the Cuban Missile Crisis.
   b. He started programs that helped America's youth fight poverty.
   c. He won the election of 1960 by a very narrow margin.
   d. He was from Massachusetts.

2. If two sides of a four-sided figure are parallel but the other two sides are not, that figure is a:
   a. triangle
   b. trapezoid
   c. perpendicular
   d. parallelogram

3. All of the following are Greek letters EXCEPT:
   a. Epsilon
   b. Delta
   c. Pi
   d. summary

4. What is true about the election of 1960?
   a. John F. Kennedy won by a landslide.
   b. Richard Nixon won the election.
   c. John F. Kennedy won by a narrow margin.
   d. Jimmy Carter won the election.

5. In the story you read, what is true about the main character, Elizabeth, in relation to her love interest, Mr. Darcy?

   a. she is always angry with Mr. Darcy.

   b. She is often angry with Mr. Darcy.

   c. She is never angry with Mr. Darcy.

   d. She has no concern with Mr. Darcy.

Answers and explanations:

1. b. Even if you don't know anything about President Kennedy, you have to find an answer that could plausibly, or believably, explain why he was popular. Being involved in a crisis of any sort—particularly a missile crisis—would not lead to his increased popularity. In addition, winning the election by a small margin shows his initial lack of popularity. Finally, being from Massachusetts isn't relevant to his popularity in the country as a whole, leaving you with only one plausible reason: he encouraged idealism about American youth to solve one of the country's most difficult problems—poverty.

2. b. Note that the question asks for a four-sided figure. A triangle has three sides (and has no parallel sides). "Perpendicular" isn't a shape. "Parallelogram" might be an answer choice, but it means all sides are parallel, so even if you didn't know what a parallelogram was, you might be able to guess from its name that it's not the right answer because not all sides of the shape described in the question are parallel. Hence, the right answer is the only choice that remains—trapezoid.

3. d. This question is fairly easy, but it asks about something you most likely don't know—Greek letters. Note that all the answer choices are capitalized as Greek letters except the last choice, an English word. You can just choose the word you've heard of or choose the answer that isn't like the others because this is an "EXCEPT" question that is looking for the exception among the answer choices.

4. c. Note that this question refers to an earlier question and that the earlier question gives you the answer. The first question already told you that John F. Kennedy won the election of 1960 by a narrow margin. On some tests, answer choices may be incorrect, but this information is correct. Reading the rest of the answers on the test may refresh your memory about the fact that Kennedy actually did win the election of 1960 by a narrow margin.

5. b. This question refers to the book *Pride and Prejudice* by Jane Austen. Even if you haven't done your reading, you should realize that Elizabeth most likely has some concern for her love interest, so d can't be the right answer. Remember that extreme answers are often not right, so Elizabeth is often angry at Mr. Darcy—but not always or never.

Exercise #5: Following written directions.

Read all the directions before beginning this test.

Draw a large circle.

Draw a square within the circle.

Write your name on the top of the circle.

Write your name within the square.

Draw lines from each side of the square to the circle.

Fold the paper in half.

Cancel all the directions above and hand in your paper without a mark on it.

Exercise #6: Test Workshop.

Have students bring in a recent test on which they did not score as well as they would have liked. Have them fill out the checklist below from Chapter 11 and come up with potential strategies for the next test.

_____ I made a lot of careless mistakes, for example in math.
   Potential strategies: _____

_____ I read the directions incorrectly.
   Potential strategies: _____

_____ I simply didn't understand the material, though I thought I did.
   Potential strategies: _____

_____ I wrote a sloppy essay exam that included bad grammar and spelling.

Potential strategies: _____

_____ I simply ran out of time.

Potential strategies: _____

Other pitfalls and strategies:_____

What I did right:_____